Call Her Triumphant

Qui Michelle

First Printing: 2021

Revised Printing: 2023

Published by Qui Michelle, LLC

ISBN 9780578893914

Library of Congress Control Number 2021909969

For further information

www.iamoyemi.com

www.instagram.com/iamoyemi

www.facebook.com/iamoyemi

www.tiktok.com/iamoyemi

www.twitter.com/iamoyemi

Dedication

To the beautiful and soulful vessel that birthed me and cheered me on.
Mom. This is in honor of you and your strengths.
I love you
I gained an Ancestor.
I love you!
Always

Mrs. Fine Wine
Strong
Capable
Bold
Mother Earth to all creation
You are valued.
You are loved.
From one Goddess to another Goddess
Flex on them!

Ase

Table of Contents

I

Am

TRIUMPHANT!

Some things you experience up close or at a distance.
Did you learn the lessons that it was teaching?
The lessons became blessings; They were the first challenges or obstacles. They are not meant to break you but build you.
I know it, however, at times I questioned whether was it worth it.

The only way to conquer it is through it.

We need trials so we can have a testimony of our triumph!

The student

Introduction

Let us explore the definition of triumphant which means ***"being met with a challenge; having won a battle and being victorious.".***

Call Her Triumphant is not a self-help or spiritual book. Although within these pages lay some ongoing learning of lessons and words not verbalized but only given my actions. I am forever a student learning that it is the right actions that make you triumphant. Each page is a triumph whether mental, physical, or psychological. The greatest battle is the one you have within and when you conquer that battle. Then you are victorious.

I chose the title because it was only fitting to do so. I once said to a person that ***"When you have been down so long; all you can do is look up so you can stand up"!*** That is the most realist statement I have ever said or wrote, and I stay saying some real shit! The battle is not what some are ready for or want. You can win or you can die physically. However, death is not just physical! It is
mental, emotional, psychological, etc. So, my ego, pride, relationships, old beliefs, and other traumatic events that I repeated and re-played in my head also had to die! Death is transformation. So yes, ***Call Her Triumphant!***

As women, we go through so much shit. Society has labeled us the bearing of all that we can handle and go at it in a hypervigilant manner and at times alone. We are to keep up our appearances because the box tells us that what we see in the mirror isn't enough so put on the look, makeup, and clothing to still be degraded and still say, "I got it" and be silently dismissed. We take on so much from the world when the world should be thanking us for creating it.

We aren't represented accurately in life at all. Period! To; the Gods and Goddesses that love us in all our glory; Thank You.

When not-so-great things happen to you; you become triumphant by using it as your ammunition and power. I use mine as ammunition and weapons. The power comes as no secret nor do I hide it. Speaking metaphorically or maybe not! What was sent to harm you or break you; you took it and made it your strength. You took action even if it felt like a small move. It was grand if it's not what you would have normally done before, smart move.

You are triumphant over a relationship, friendship, family, life, and the unfolding that includes being let down and so much more. However, your biggest boss move is intentionally leveling up and knowing more about yourself. You started mentally.

Within these pages I hold nothing back; not even myself. Some of these poems are in the moment and in real-time. If you have chosen, this book or it chose you then; may it give you all the ammunition you need to make the change to be Triumphant or re-enforce in you what you already know. You are the phenomenal, life-giving Goddess you
embody!

Ase, Ase, Ase O!

Peace and Love!

Oyemi

I Can Swim

Allow my words to capture you and not drown you like to me; you tried to do.
You see; tides come in waves and my waves are hitting the shore continuously and effortlessly.
It's high tide now and all I see is my home while radiating overflow.
My elevator door doesn't fit the standard and traditional.
I make leaps and bounds quietly.
Wipe the spill with a Bounty; I have quick reflexes and my arsenal is my ancestry.
I said what I said.
Voodoo doesn't create people like you, but life do.
Some people will move, adapt, or stay living and being the same and they refuse to change.
Quick to talk about a vision and get mad when ain't no one else believing it and still plotting or hating on other niggas pockets.
Gas you up just to ghost you when they can't get a train to run you through.
They called me a failure.
But I forgot I Can Swim

You mimic like seagulls when they see food; they hover and gawk.
When I heard you speak long enough, I learned your talk.
Your game is what I initially bought.
My codependency habits: I grew into from the last few, no excuse.
On my clock, I hit the snooze because I thought I needed them
One because I was bored, one to make me laugh, the other I wanted to wife up and one became another lesson then I learned I had to stop.
I am honest with myself so let my truth be the word that is heard.
I Can Swim

Shore ahead
The tides talked smoothly, but I had no plan once I hit land.
I laugh at myself because the shit is true.
However, no one deserves to worry about where they are going to lay their head next!

Shit stinks when the same crew that sent for you hits the pilot auto-eject.
Leaving you isolated
Treated me like a reject
I had forgotten I was Ariel from Under the Sea.
I am now effectively using my legs.
Fishing nets down and the catch is all free game.
I was birthed by Yemoje who reigns with Olokun.
My ancestral mothers
Now I know why I love to get beach wet and side quiet moments away from others.
I Can Swim

You pushed me out of the boat.
Said *'Find your way yourself.'*
Now I am politely singing *FUCK YOU* on the keynote.
I watched you veer off right before sunset.
I was left with no life vest.
I was going down in distress as I watched you speed away.
Shit hurt me to my heart that this was coming from a fake ass hombre!
Water in my lungs and I asked myself *"What have I become"?*
My body remembered and I grew gills that replaced my ribs.
My tail was strong and from the nets I became uncaught.
I recall your ways in an afterthought!
I can walk and I Can Swim

Tragedy is on you because your access has been foreclosed.
Your true character shows.
You shaded me like Sombreros.
Your leaving me to drown miles on the coast was the best thing you did!
I'm the daughter of Yemoje.
A toast is what I propose; manifiesto.
I did that. I still Rose

Triumphant

I wear battle marks and battle scars as armor to be proud of!
Call it *"I made it"!*
The muscles obtained came from challenges that only enlightened my body.
I had a samurai lay their sword down in my honor.
Bow down in the presence of a Queen.
From the nations that speak Swahili, Yoruba, Xhosa, and Zulu
At times I felt that I couldn't and wouldn't continue.
Everything on the outside isn't what it appears or seems.
I have faith, a vision, and belief running through my bloodstream.
I have open spaces.
I stopped stumbling on the bumps in the road and got a surreal map to follow.
The intuition of my own
In emotions, for too long I didn't wallow
The pain felt like lava had run through my veins.
Fire and flames had me seeing red they said it was Shango.
Spreading like a wildfire
Until it rained with the winds of Oya
Once the smoke extinguished; I came out with better dedication.
No oxygen deprivation
Just more motivation
Serving gravy with my self-infatuation
Not trying to sound redundant.
So, I'll keep it to the facts.
I am triumphant!

Fuck You Mean

Fuck you mean?
Really, what do you mean?
Please don't fuck with me.
No handouts were given and those that were; were opportunities.
I had to maneuver amongst hungry and thirsty sharks.
Manipulating; baiting, self-hating, and unhappy folks
The waters were pitch black and dark.
No ropes, life vest, or savers. No rescue team came with boats.
That was too easy.
You see me and wanna sit at my table.
Let me school you before you grab yourself a plate.
I am a victorious survivor of one out of three
I was young and that old ass man touched me.
Yea, I am outing that nigga.
My mouth won't be silenced by some form of a distorted mentality, nor will I conform.
I still hope he changes.
Eugene is his name.
I told his new wife, too! Strength is what I have reclaimed.
I have loved, hated, and resented for so long on so many.
Those moments in life I had, I have dealt with and some are forgiven within, and I had to extend forgiveness to myself foremost.
Inner self, inner child I console her.
She is my new black wealth.
The darkness comes in a variety of forms from people, and we rumbled closely!
Oh, you didn't know they can shapeshift.
I have been healing and reviving myself and saying I am safe, stable, secure and balanced.
I'm just stating it and bringing you up to speed.
I am showing up more importantly for me.
Perseverance, and mental clearance at times mingle but I embody endurance.
I put it down at times only to pick it right back up.
Yeah, a break is fundamental; this doesn't come with a prenup.
There had been a lockdown with a Quarantine.

So, what the fuck do you mean?
You got an excuse!
When there was nothing else to do but work on you!

No Matter the Age we all still have dreams ready to be birthed and lived in too!

The first thing is to stop making fucking excuses on why you didn't do that thing you wanted to do! The only person who can stop you is you!

Lack creates opportunities to get creative.
-Tobe Calls Me Fat

Who Am I?

Remind me; who am I?
I didn't realize that apparently when I left you; I left her too.
She smiles, sings, she lights up dim rooms.
But I found them stagnant.
I had to face all my demons and the darkness alone.
They wait and reside; they don't hide.
I now got them traumatized by what I can do.
They gave her armor that was weighted to keep her down.
I no longer carry the weights but still have the heat, but I haven't used it yet.
Does metal rust even in its sheath?
Can a woman be rebirthed into a beauty queen after being the black sheep?
I am ready to sit back, sip chill, and flex these muscles and skills.
Allow my success and progress to show how I became skilled.
I want a love that recognizes me.
Mimics me and/or surpasses me in frequencies.
I wanna learn from one another.
Whatever I don't know.
I want you to teach me.
Let's laugh uncontrollably!

Then for a slight moment
I caught myself chanting
Because I am gratefully expecting.
I realize now I am more accepting
I start first by looking at me in the mirror!
Things have gotten clearer
I guess I no longer need glasses or contacts!
To see the bigger picture

Is Depression Winning?

They keep saying I am resilient!
Lately, I ain't feeling it.
Depression yea I know... but not like this tho.
She is dark and at times will not talk.
A ride to a ledge along the raging seas
Just me and my running thoughts
I just wanted my body to land wherever she decided to go.
Then I hear "*If something happens to you then who's gonna take care of me?*"
Real shit!
Leaving behind the only real one.
I did have a plan to a point.
Living day by day without a permanent foundation is no easy task to do.
I was homebound without having a "too" physical address.
That meant I was homeless.
You never knew it
I was washing dishes in our hotel sinks.
Felt like going back to the seas that kept calling me.
Scaring myself
Sitting with these private thoughts alone
Only the divine and ancestors here me calling in English,
Spanish and a language I did not recognize but I understood.
"Ayuda me! No sé si puedo hacerlo
Ahorita en mi menta tengo los suenas de yo muerto
Pero, yo no quiero"
The "*I got you*" I heard far too many times.
To me, it's just another overused pickup line
Is the battle taking over?
The thoughts I could tell no one.
There was no one I could talk to who could relate.
There was no "so let's sit down and conversate".
So, on this page, I can express them here.
No judgment; not even from my pen
Isolated and not by choice or Covid
Can resilience save me?
From preparing,

Wondering, contemplating, and fighting
This a foreign type of depression!

Dear, depression.
Bitch: I demand that you let me go
You are getting way out of control.
Let me go..........
.....................Let me go
Root chakra, Sacral chakra!
So, your question to me now "*Is depression winning or are you winning?*"
I wanna say ask me later after I get sativa and I've meditated!
However, since I am talking about her.
I give her acknowledgment.
I have courage; so, I say
I am winning!

You Give Me Chills

Oh, My Goodness
Well; damn!
You give me chills.
This ain't the coochie throb type or a one-night stand
Hit it off right but not before my bite!
No; this ain't even about a person!
Unless we are talking in the third person
Then fuck Yea that would be me
I'm sitting here days wondering why I am getting excited within my body
It can be intense or subtle
No cold chill although it's chilly I got the fire pit lit and I'm sitting in front of it
You have angles, you have spaces, you have unlimitedness written all over you
So who am I talking to?
I am talking to you; the one with the pen
I'm gravitated by your pull and determination
Congratulations on all your achievements and accomplishments
There's so much about you that in others I haven't run across
But I swear I know when I do
No introductions when you stare at your reflection enhanced, upgraded, fine as ever, lavish couture beauty, hersome
Looking right at you
You give me chills
I'm sitting with you at the traffic light and the way your light radiates
A look in the mirror and you smiling like
SHIT I DID THIS
Looking at the flames dancing towards me because they too wanna be extra lit
Girl, you've silently been doing big shit

With no permanent address but a PO Box that's solid
When you look around you; your elevations and heights are bigger.
Seen things you dreamed and experienced each of them likes and dislikes.
Forging ahead in life
I am just talking about you.
I gotta give it up to you Queen.
I love the way you smirk on the left side of your mouth It Is putting emphasis on your right-sided mole
That's you looking at you in the mirror.
It's not a wonder why
I give myself chills

Silence

You ask for the
T R U T H
A lie is what you rendered from what I say.
Asking about justice and I guess maybe, possibly it'll happen once.
D
A
Y
My skin must not be light enough.
Maybe there's truth in what they say!
That this melanin doesn't matter as much anyway
My full lips were not thin enough but they speak.
L O U D L Y

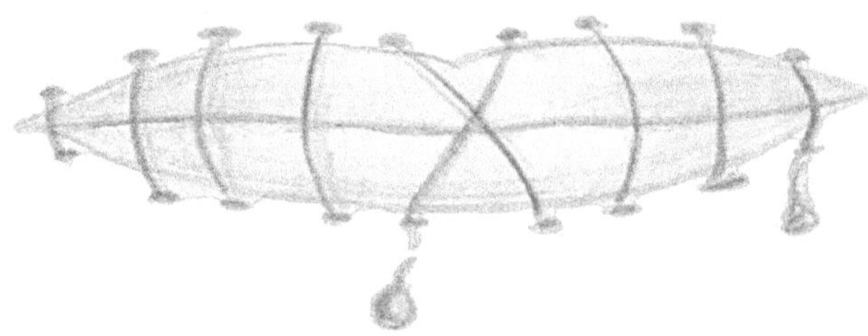

You tried to drown me out from baring truths and the stories that I was told to not ever speak.
Scriptures of pain and resilience have been tattooed on my epidermis for centuries.
Deep-rooted ink!
Embedded from the words you turn away.
My eyes have seen things that as an adult still ricochet.
My fingers feel, my brain thinks and
I wonder are you really checking for me?
My voice is loud and I say, *"Does my life matter?"*
How about my story?
More importantly ARE YOU READY FOR IT?
Tell me to my face.
Does my life matter?
I say it does which is why we are here now, so let's communicate.

Dirty Laundry

Before I can pour into someone else

I must pour from my overflow and provide for myself first.

So, pour me another.
Caramel Brule latte with Oat milk with Agave syrup
Or a green juice with ginger and Elderberry
I am way more mature and open-minded and I see clearly.

Yes, it was unhealthy.
The words spoken, "*You don't do it for me.*"
were better than being single.
I knew that no matter what I did; my good wasn't enough.
Then I got a letter from myself when I had Sativa and it spoke
"*I am way too good for this.*"
I heard and I learned.

The dirty laundry
Didn't get clean in the first of many few cycles.
They ended the same.
Only further faded.
So, what happens when things begin to repeat?
The breakdowns
Got too familiar.
And you can predict the outcome!
It was a cycle for me that had to end.
You get new everything; change the soap and obtain a new machine.
Then give it a new run.
Now I realize
The greatest hurt to myself was knowing and still ignoring.
When the dirty laundry piles and they are too soiled to get clean
The dirt was deeper and still stained after I used Oxy Clean.
On that ass, I did my version of a Waiting to Exhale
Burned it all up like Bernadine.

Yo, this is so real. Cycles repeat and they don't end until you acknowledge them. They repeat and repeat until you see the pattern. As they repeat, they get grimier that is until when your vision for change, changes.

"What doesn't come out of the wash comes out the rinse."

– Nas (No Negative Energy)

If that does not work well donate it, trash it, or burn it safely. Sometimes the dirty laundry is you.
The intrusive thoughts that get you so caught up.
So, clean up your mind.
Either way, it must go!

From Afar

When fears are bigger than the truth
When a secret is better than any lie no one wants to see proof.
I know I am not alone in this fight!
Someone said to me:
"Be you and embrace your truths, love yourself more than they love you."
I now understand that at times their pain and their secrets are bigger than
the past that they dare not speak.
We all have stories.
But I ain't the type to search for your solution; not anymore.
I step on my toes, close those doors, throw away the key, and send prayers to those few who can't find their own words or power.
This is the shine you can't dim.
One day when they are ready, they allow their diaphragm to expand and the tongue finds the words that will only leave from out their mouth!
Directed up about every issue; May they find the courage.
Acknowledge their absolution.
No waiting from me; I demolish bridges purposely.

I can love them all from afar or not at all!

Journal Entry
July 2020

I do not have to have negative people around me. Whether they are family, friends, or exes, we just met, if they helped me in a significant way, or if we must occupy the same space.

If the energy not
fitting for me and depletes me. Then I will gladly let it/them go. I have been through too much to have to bend for
others who refuse to bend or support me.

I learned that there are times I must love people from afar or not at all.
With no regrets!

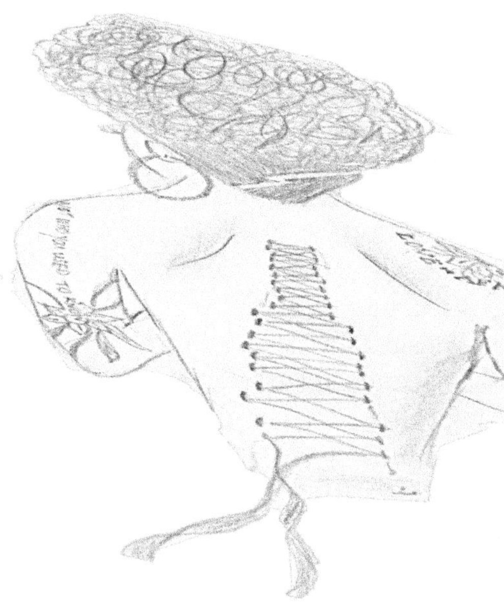

Ties That Don't Bind

What is a family?
When a family ain't been a
family to me
I've cursed out a few for not
staying in their place.
Everybody has an opinion when
they assume you failing but
cinched lips when you are
handling business
I've never seen a bunch of
spiritually dead folks walking
among the living.
Help you just to talk about you!
Talk about what they don't know!
I realize the reason why there
are buried secrets.
A matriarch that's one-sided and
Still holding onto bitterness
There remains so many.
Hypocrites.
Bitterness will kill eve-
ry.
dream if you give it your energy.
So, I am instinctively staying
away.
It's a smart move.
Those generational cycles don't
break until you break them for
you!
I acknowledge their patterns and
even the ones in me.
I refuse to settle for less, I am too
stubborn!
I don't mind severing ties,
And parting ways.
When those same ties pulled back
the life raft.
Someone tell them that I rose up
and now I am sailing smooth.

April 2019

Fearless

All because I took my lead.
They say I am reckless and dangerous.
That is from those who don't know me!
However, it depends on what aspect you are looking at.
I just say I am courageous.
Standing firm and rooted in my position because I overcame fear.
At times I have doubted myself and other times I cheered for myself
Fighting through and back tears
It was just me!
I would rather take a chance than no chance at all.
I would rather jump and leap.
not sit.
There never was a fall!
I stand up and occasionally I put my hands on my hips.
I will give the "it's the hip and side butt view."
No fighting all I could do was submit to something bigger than my view.
I leaped in and landed on my feet.
Every vision I own I invest in
Starting with me first
No more back seat, passenger riding.
I am present and I take the lead.
Are you watching this shift?
We are succeeding.
Where are you standing?

They Not Checking On You

I love people who like to check on me through other people.
"How is she doing?"
You got my number just pick up and call to see.
People will make up every excuse because they didn't and couldn't call you.
So, allow me to fill you in since you want to know.
I was depressed and thought about suicide.
I tried but somehow was sparred.
I cried and hated myself and my condition.
But that was then.
Now I am good
I am living, loving myself, and embracing all my beauty marks.
Come back, pull back, snatch back game on real strong!
When you see me keep that same energy!
Remember you do not know me!
You see misery loves misery!
Misery will have you getting the wrong kind of attention and redirecting your mission!
Are you settling for someone or something?
Got you checking on me prematurely not sincerely.
Got you holding grudges from years ago.
But I bet you don't remember why though!
Got you putting up a front that you are happy, but you are living on the edge.
Like the old folks say, you lie in it.
You made your bed.
See I am happy, genuinely happy!
Happiness is not about the space or place you reside in.
It's about what's inside!

Ask yourself if your misery is providing comfort for you.

Leaving

I know you wondering what I am thinking!
Wondering what I am contemplating!
What is behind those doors that you cannot see or perhaps you just refuse too.
I have already left mentally.
I am packed up and ready to go physically.
No longer waiting patiently on you, I am physically moving.
I could not stay there.
Existing and truly unhappy
The power and the force of your bashing and harsh words
Trying to stab and break me.
You stayed attached to your exe who was a co-signee.
I was alone, isolated, and depleted. You became my only friend as I had no one to turn to. So, no I will not stay.
Especially not for you!
That is what happens when people are through.
There is no room in the space that has been ripped and mended.
far too many times.
When a *"You don't know us"* is not comprehended
It got too crowded for the negativity, the toxic co-dependency, the little interaction with my child, and the behaviors I had gotten used to.
I was settling.
I deserve to create a life of all things beautiful and fun.
I am love and peace.
I am joyful.
More importantly, I rise as an entire good vibe.
I understood and made peace with the fact you are not the one.
A glimpse of me is what you see.
When my presence leaves; now I finally think of me and mini me and we left completely free.

November 2019

Attachments

I was attracted to you.
Your smile, your touch, and your caress
Compared to those before you, yours felt the best!
What was hidden I could see but I blindly chose to proceed.
Not blaming you
So, I digress

I laid my best and openness to you.
At your feet, I laid my solitude
Neglecting my priorities
including my seed
You never asked me to, but I did.
just to meet your needs.
Expectations to live up to what I knew.
I couldn't fulfill.
But still, I tried too.

I was going crazy, acting irrationally,
keying cars and praying
that I don't end up behind bars or worse catch a major case
Who was I?
I knew.
Feeling the pull of a separation that was needed.
However.
At times, the mind is weak.
Looking for signs but many signs said to leave, but I stayed.
You said, "*Don't rule us out.*"
Grateful we never sworn in when your home is no longer our house.

Remember?
You called us ungrateful.
I guess you forgot when I held down two car notes, rent, auto insurance, expenses and paid for our trips, and allowed you to quit a job while I was battling something medically unknown.
Greetings with open arms and a smile made me feel special
That is some cold-hearted and scary shit
So, I took take several seats away.
Got more into me.
I let go of you!
Mentally, emotionally, and physically
No order.
It's not love if we are too attached.
Real love does not hurt.
Our attachments do

I used to think that love was this fancy feeling of butterflies and that with it I would feel extraordinary.
Those butterflies were my high and I chased it daily.

No one told me that too much of anything is an addiction. I was addicted to being loved in the wrong way and that always led to hard feelings, life lessons, a cold bed, wet pillows, and being alone.

One day I read somewhere that love is never supposed to hurt but an attachment does!

I am no longer attached, just attached more to my growth. The way it should always be.

Life is a continuous cycle of letting in and letting go.
The flow!
It is the learning of lessons.
Letting go of what I was so attached to made me more confident to let go of everything that was no longer serving a divine purpose in my life.
Seasons do not become trees, but their lessons are seasons you learn from.
You bloom through them
No matter what the attachment is; I let it go to receive what provides a more healthy way for growth!

So, what are you attached to?

Hindsight Part 1

Three years after we first met.
You were taken and I was single!
Out of respect for your girl, you cut contact off
Two years later you were single, and I was involved.
You tried but I denied it.
Talking to you made things so complex.
Pushing you away was what I had to do.
I was confused because I truly did want you.
I should have loved you like a metaphor.
Find places and phrases just to include you more.
Maybe you would've completed this sentence.
You're the one I let get away.
This is something you should have known.
You would have if I told you so.
Yet again because of loyalty and my ego, I let you go.
I wanted my exe; crazy I know.
We didn't make it to the next anniversary.
I moved on.
So, I tried to find you.
I searched Facebook, and Messenger and I even searched for you on a legal site.
I did locate you.
Just didn't feel right intervening in whatever in your life was new
Maybe you would think I was stalking you.
True... True
Letters to your P.O. Box may not have been received well.
If it was still accurate
Ok; yes, that is obsessive however just for a moment let's stay!
focused and overlook that! Lol.
I was desperate in a "what do I do"?
I wanted what I denied myself to experience; that is all of you
I had to just leave it alone and let you be.
I should have accepted all your advances even the last time I saw you in the parking lot!
Nothing is random but I ran into you at the IHOP.
I should have hopped into your arms because your few words felt
Sacred.
"Hey, what's up?"
As you passed by me your waft, your aura, your presence was peace.

Pride and disappointment in myself overcame me.
A fluid conversation until I again pushed you away and spoke.
"I want to get back with my ex."
Although she had already left and was miles and states distance from me
I overlooked YOU standing in front of me.
I should have kept our emails and texts.
I wanted to go back at times and just reconnect.
Hindsight: honestly, I wasn't with the right one
How did I miss the damn signs that YOU were either the one or the one redirecting me from the wrong one?
I wish you well though.
In the end, I was left with the what if of possibilities that I would never know.
I remember when you spoke of
babies, marriage and me being your wife.
Music bells to my ears but I was in a complicated situation.
I mean I was in a relationship!

Yeah: real mature and healthy love used to scare me
But my exe and I had history!
I didn't know that the stars were aligning me to you.
An opportunity that I should have taken!
A life with the person that could have been right.
You were the "sign" from the divine
I've already said too much so I won't say no more.
However,
Hindsight.
I believe it was you that at that point in my life, I had always prayed for!

"Shy" September 2018

We keep people in our lives past our and their learning experience. Missing out on the one you were meant for. A person can never know the possibilities if they stay holding onto someone or something that is displaying no connection.
Just ask me!
Without half-assing it. We have outgrown.
Love is no race. Time is to not be wasted though because we can never escape it so don't waste it.
Believe in by-chance encounters. Embrace the signs given to us by the Universe.
Only you can interpret them.
You never know what can be by missing or passing by on opportunities or genuine and sincere people.
Especially the ones you know you deserve.

Cherish people in their presence or you will feel their absence.

Never take someone's affection, love, or time for granted, and never waste another's time if their presence isn't desired.

Listen to you and your heart. The grass can be greener on the other side if it's tended, watered, and nurtured. It can grow. Better, produce more nourishment and be more plentiful than your neglected and unmanicured lawn!
Dead lawns can only regrow; but how long has it been neglected?

For me, that other lawn was greener, better, and tended to nicely, I was just too afraid to let go of history!
Now I know!

Journal Entry September 2018

Underneath

Satin sheets and pillows
Burned until there were no remnants, and it left a stench.
Where we laid, laughed, made love, loved, argued, and where we finally last parted.
So strange how an "*I Love You*" can be so still!
Yet still do not feel any more real
Not sure if it's hatred, blame, or sadness.
You weren't all I had, I just placed it all in you
Remember; when you said, *"You need me, I'm all ya'll got"*.
The Most High created us a way to escape.
So, what lies beneath burned sheets?
Ashes, dried tears, final goodbyes, and a now hard silence.
Dart stares and laughs to cover the pain being hidden from the feeling.
For me it's *FUCK YES,* I am ready
I have forgiveness for you even though you feel it's not needed.
My happiness starts with me first being clear-headed!
By first undoing what's been created

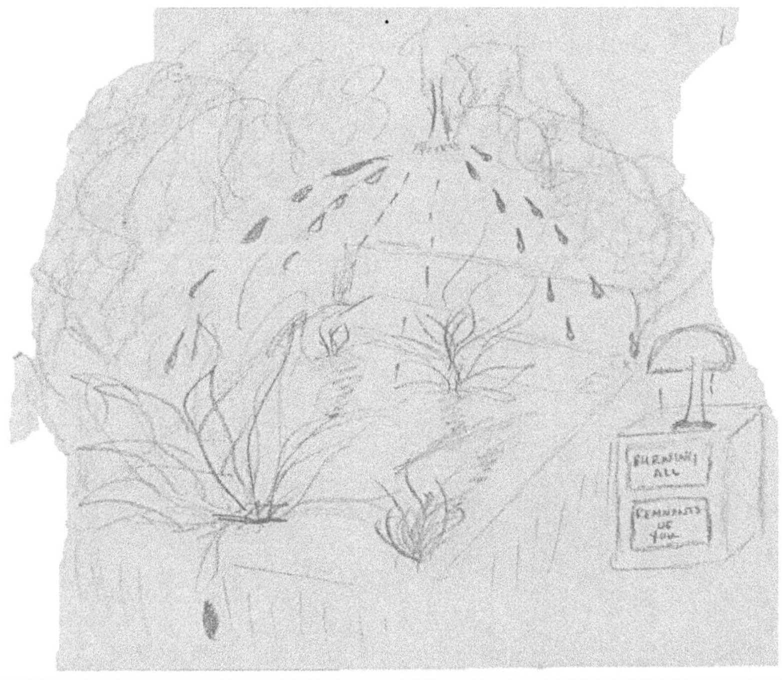

Hindsight Part 2

I was so used to making the wrong decisions

That the right decisions at times felt wrong

So, I rejected quite a few of them.

What would a few years of happy memories and mostly happy tears with

you have been like or felt like?

Instead, we got breakups, makeups that we just kept repeating

I don't know

That's why
I am doing what should have been done months into a relationship that
lasted for years too many

I am letting go of
YOU!

September 2019

You

Helpful, kind, a gentlewoman, a pleaser
Open doors for you because that's what you do
Some of the best displays of affection I ever had
I am so grateful I got to experience you

Deep beyond all your flaws
In every capacity
There are so many lessons and teachings
I got all that from learning through you
You did what you thought you needed to do
You forgot that the package deal
Will always include two!
Not accepting that will make me leave

Unseated

I told you my plans and you were silent?
I told you that everything I envisioned was manifesting.
You kept quiet.
I got no congratulations.
When I needed help you said you were *"too busy"*
Remember when we spoke about us being here?
I said I did not want to do this without you.
I thought that's what you wanted, too.
I was left to drown by the ones who knew me most.
So, I am not here to brag or boast.
On your behalf allow me to propose a toast
Thank You
You all helped me transform.
I learned how to be quiet, and I received big blessings
Silent abundance and silent prosperity but I get loud with my gratitude shouts
and praises because I am showing my appreciation.

I am here without you.
In case you are inquiring; Yes.
I filled your seat with someone else silently too.

Free Birds

Comfort is good but I prefer peace.
Bullet formats can never define me.
Exceptions and expectations
Idealism is cool however what's better than opportunities?
I am a free bird!
Clip her wings and they will find her.
Bury her and she will find her way out.
Drown her and she will still find oxygen.
Try to suffocate her and she will still breathe.
So
Allow her to blossom and let her go.

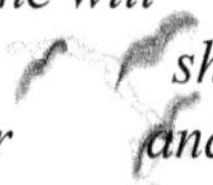

Free birds need room.

She will make an open and inviting space her home.

Watch her, adore her, and admire her and she'll give it right back!

Restrict her and it is a full-on attack!

She must be unhindered when the world is here
almanac

They call her an open flame
Goes where the wind blows
Free spirits can't be tamed

Instrumental

This beat is instrumental.
I represent the energy of the feminine universal.
Allow the blood to pump and bleed out the pain like a female menstrual.
Life is essential
Growth is never incidental
Light it up, sit back, and LOVE me up like a musical
I love you like sheet music
You are part of my melody
Your flow is my tempo
We are like Black Monday, and I am Regina King
I Spiritually kill my ego.
That B had to get a wake-up call.
She moved up into the mountains and got choked up and decapitated.
No worries though; she had to go.
No remorse
I just enforce my force because my peace is real.
Better believe I still carry that steel.
Believe me, the Oya will give you the wind with a body!
Not one you can feel.
My spirits say don't test me when these winds are tornadoes
That'll put you on your toes.
Shoot you like a precise arrow.
I also nurture your soul.
The fuel in ya jet
Your cheerleader on and off-set
I offset the beat
I would take the steps still just to know how aligned I am with you
Dancing to the sound of your feet
Peace my name is Oyemi!
It's nice to finally meet you.

Space

Torn between a full heart and a clouded mind.
Thinking maybe just maybe we could give it another try.
Another time
Yet .... again
Didn't matter what was happening.
Didn't matter how bad we were unraveling.
I guess that's what happens when it's with someone you're used to.
I said I wasn't.
I didn't until I left.
In your real absence
The after moment
Reality set in and I cried multiple times.
Thinking maybe I should go back.
Maybe it was a mistake.
That was all confusion in an illusion mixed with our toxicity.
That I got so fucking used to
So, there is no more trying or going back to cross a blurred line.
Emotions run high and wild when you find your heart in a reluctant place.
So, I followed my heart and she shouted for
Space

Some Kinda Love

What could have been us?
2,035 days
That is 2,035 pictures I went through.
Videos too
At times I had multiple pictures in one day
Moments, times, recollections, and impressions
no more emotional suppressions
My tears poured out your name for every year, day, second, and every minute.
Holidays that replay like the day you surprised us with a Christmas tree.
When you went all out for my birthday
Putting out in your way
It is memories on this page where I will last reminisce.
I deleted and erased all pics.
Cropped and edited you out.
No more waits, pauses, or rewinds
I do not care for a reset or replay
It is gonna stay that way

Change Up

Ever been amid a presence brought on by your
existence
See, I've been around so much fake.
I could make a quilt made from their guilt.
I no longer try to align with any print if it doesn't fit.
You have to be careful not to keep people past their due date.
That was my own mistake.
To see clearly; their access to me became closed.
People will use bro, sis, bae, and boo on you quickly.
Be cautious though.
They will call you by your name when they no longer need you.
They knead in the fakery.
That is when it's time to call it quits.
I will give it a name and call it the Mastery in Bakery.
I have learned this through my own experiences.
I am real enough to acknowledge their bait and wise enough to
Accept the mastery of my fate!
That which alone I co-create
It is never in the minds of others but that of my own.
It is not how they see me.
Only in how I see myself.
I let them change up.
I giveaway, walk away, and have my bags packed.
I call in the haulers to come clean up.
Facts

Holidays

I pulled out the ornaments today.
I cried!
This year there will be no Christmas with you.
Our last holiday played the way it should have always been.
Peaceful and in sync
That was always the
MISSING LINK
That's when I knew I had peace and could leave
The first time we maneuvered.
Like a family except we never became one.
I love to celebrate holidays and those to come without you.

December 22, 2019

Sis

I am certain we ain't the same people.
About face – right face – two face – multiple faces
I feel like I can slap a chick in the face in this place.
I have watched your moves, actions, words, and your plays.
Sis came with false intentions which is a low blow.
See; sis ain't a sis around here.
It is chatter but you not breaking bread when you are forced to make the batter.
Sis cannot keep it real, but I can keep it loose.
Fists can come up like they used to.
For what though, what you did ain't nothing new.
It is just new to feel it so close especially coming from you
Especially coming from you.
State your thesis
Come up with a hypothesis and let us see if it all fits!
Fighting people off like shock from sepsis
With me, there are no second chances
I closed tight like anaphylaxis.
Dealers don't deal the same hand twice.
So, I took that same energy and blessed it into the cake.
I left you the icing and the spoon to lick.
No regrets
I am so glad I left *"Sis"* so quickly.

I listen to people.

I notice a person's actions.

I ask about their intentions.

I read them.

I also listen to the spirit when my back is turned

And what a person doesn't say

However, I measure their truth by their body language and

Iwa Pele (Good Character).

FACTS!

The Last

I don't play guessing games.
I do eliminations.
Purge and remove all toxicity.
Spiritual cleansing of my body and throwing away what doesn't de-
serve to occupy my space.
I took a deep breath of fresh air and I felt serene.
I am finally free.
Took back what everyone thought was taken from me.
I am light years,
I fly here.
I call on the Divine and cover myself throughout time.
I cut out the meat and incorporated plants.
This is my new language and I don't expect you to understand.
I ignore your advances.
I put that to an end.
I learned from you which is why there are no second chances.

Salt Water

In the confusion, the mess, and the chaos
I tried to stay afloat.
Not aware of myself
Only the sharks that were surrounding me
I was bleeding tremendously.
It was just space and empty seas.
I floated for a minute.
I didn't know I could swim.
I was left to the dangers of what lies beneath.
The mental pics could have done me in
I was left for dead intentionally.
I said fuck it and I just allowed myself to
Let go.
Then I grew into a mermaid with a tailfin and
That became the ……

I needed and wanted!

I Give Up

To the idea of what you expect me to be
I gave up on every insecurity I allowed to haunt me.
The feelings, I did not acknowledge properly
To your perception of me, that doesn't validate my being
To deny my happiness.
To not express myself accurately.
To anyone who does not see my vision.
As long as I do, that's all that's needed.
I give up on allowing negativity to surround me.
Trying to fit you into my path and my vision.
This is my mission.
I give up chasing people who are not running towards me.
Run Forest, run 'cause I'm not running after you!

If you cannot catch up, I won't wait.
I don't slow down
Those are risks I no longer take.
I give up, I am fed up
I am open to all the opportunities.
I give in to my ideas, my visions
To everything that makes me happy and grants me Peace.
I give in to myself and all the possibilities.

Shadow Work

Who's that creeping through the windows?
POW; nobody now!
I swore I locked it, sealed it
Didn't come through the back door
Like SWAT or the police when they looking for a suspect
She is black, fits the description and that is it
Dog sniffing all over my butt
Got that dark nose and they killed the lights but I can still see

So, I stood naked in the mirror.
Chanting affirmations
I love you to the person I no longer know.
Wrote down what was spoken.
I only prayed for a miracle.
I got shit that I can't explain but it took away the pain.
No drugs, no drinking, and no selling my soul
Oh no
Incantations that I didn't realize became invocations to the spirit.
It lightened my entire load
Got me prepared and ready for the miracles and open doors.
Removed all the obstacles out of the way.
I got quiet to hear what was spoken.
I asked for wealth, prosperity, new wealth, and like-minded friends.
I got blessed and brought the light to the dark
Michael Jackson Thriller
Michael Myers wearing a mask but he is not the killer
Assassination of dead weight and cold hearts
Leave your feelings because they came with hurt
Gutted me to my knees.
Asking for signs, honoring my pleas, and allowing me to live whole again.
I cried, I pleaded,
I realized that every time I did, all I was doing was releasing
What had to be.

It is intense and it is deep
There is profound healing when healing from the past that has tormented you.
You may begin to look for more reasons to laugh
The tears have watered your garden
Do no allow it to be overwatered with stuff you know is not growing or being reproduced for harvest
It is challenging to get used to yourself when you have hidden from you for so long.
The mirror reveals all
If you desire a new different and something more uplifting
I promise that it is not outside of you.
It starts with you
You deserve what you have denied and that is healthy love for yourself and a golden sunshine that radiates your aura.
New is scary, familiar is a predictable pattern so why not do the daring.
Get uplifted and elevated with like minded people and more importantly with empowering and helpful thoughts.

That's a win so give yourself a hand a clap and smile.

No Compromise

I gave you a choice and you wanted a compromise.
Like my time to valuable, if we not building a solid foundation then in your field I ain't playing.
What did I expect?
A homerun when there were too many foul balls.
I settled for someone that I thought I needed until I understood.
The greatest life lesson is getting what you thought you needed just to understand that it is not meant for you!
Truth be told I was afraid to be alone.
I allowed your disrespect to take over me until I forgot who I was.
But I grew up!
Realized; You were not my type!
My palate is delicate, it's not easy to digest something or someone that isn't meant for you.
I am way too light for any dark to dim.
No Compromise; right?
Stay sharp, stay focused, and cut them ties if you must!
Stop at nothing; right?
I'd rather leave you than leave myself.
I took my feelings back off the shelf.
Replanted them back inside of me.
So, the sacrifice is to never minimize yourself to a compromise that doesn't fit.

Learning as a student:

Compromising is so delicate. It requires sound judgment and Complete trust.

However, one can never compromise themselves for the sake of something that is not for you! It does not feel right.

You will lose your identity, self-esteem, and more importantly the knowledge of your worth!

Compromising should never be degrading or minimizing to you. It should feel inviting because you are MAXIMIZING and GROWING!

Anything less than that; well, deserves you to leave entirely. You deserve greatness!

Solid

No matter the situation
No matter the distance
You have been consistent.
I could call on you and get a sincere embrace from you.
I could vent to you.
You kept your problems and vented your pleas.
Two people who are experiencing their separate dramas.
Yet you still show up.
You never changed up.
When I was down you were there helping me in whatever capacity you could to stand up.
You offered me light, prayers, and a hand no matter that we ain't kin folk.
You still encourage me.
Blessing me
Not stressing me
The divine I know resides within you.
Solid people are rare.

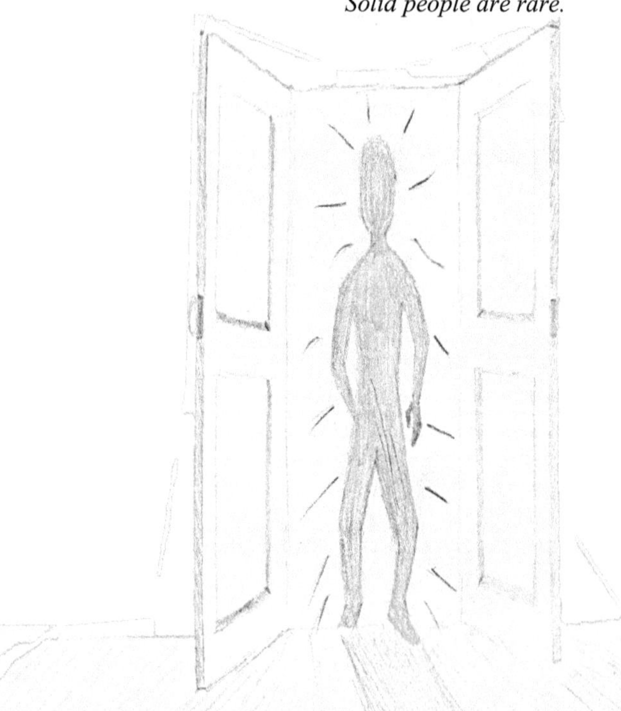

Pain, Passion, and Purpose

*Ask me about **Pain** and I will tell you how I got my jaw socked and dislocated by a man nicknamed Knox.*
I was fifteen.
He liked little girls with their chests poked out.
Moms turned a blind eye because she liked her handouts.
At twenty-one a gun barrel and trigger happy envious enemy ready to squeeze
I showed no fear and I walked up to the barrel.
headfirst and there I planted.
Begging him to honor my pleas, and please squeeze.
From this world help me leave
Or at twenty-three carrying crack in Oochie Wally because I am a down rider
Ain't no bang-bang on my end when my girl kept a clip ready, loaded, and on silent.

*Ask me about **Passion** and I got stories about how I used to make my hands bleed!*
From fighting to writing on pads, paper, or napkins because this thought has to come out.
Better these words than these hands
If we met then you know its accuracy to flesh; will land.
But these words melodize better than any symphony or beating drums.
The sky opened to come to hear me sing with words that found home.
A vision that sat silent until it was revived.
After shots were fired and I was alive

Although we can talk about pain, I am sure we will allow me to keep it trill
That pain led me to a passion and showed me I am worth so much more.
No out of the slums I already lived that.
I found that within my pain resided the passion that helped me.
*understand my **Purpose!***

No one is immune from pain.
No one is immune from discomfort.
No one is immune from passion or having a purpose.
You just must tap into it.

Pain is discomfort and can place one in survival mode.
It can also cause one to be in action or non-active.
I'm still being taught to be proactive than reactive and that didn't always work out due to my own mistakes.

I didn't know strength; I just knew the moment whatever was happening I was not going to accept it.

Call me a fighter
Call me a warrior
Call me courageous
Call me fearless
In my eyes anyone who went through any trauma or event and got through it. I call you Superhuman!

Call me Triumphant

I salute everyone who has turned their pain and within it found a passion. Aligning with your purpose!

Clarity

See people not speaking to me don't phase me!
The chatter spoken outside my presence just validates who I decide to get my guidance from
And it's not amongst those full of judgments.
I know which groups I don't belong to.
I'm real about mine and I'll tell you how I feel.
It won't be over dinner with a hot feast and a full-course meal.
I can't be fake eating with the same people who served me slop and masked it as the real deal.
I don't worry about the mass appeal.
As you watched and waited as I went through my ordeal
So, believe me; I'll cut ties and burn down bridges deliberately just to get rid of you.
Deadweight and negative energy
All ya'll are going to
The saying that says "blood is thicker than water" is untrue.
If you dilute it enough it will run thin like most people do
I can watch you pack up and head out with the biggest cheesy grin on my face.
I'll drain the river of a catastrophe and plant a bed of flowers.
as a finality
And burn my sage and Palo Santo just to keep you away.
Oh, what clarity brings
Don't let your eyes fool you into what you think you see!
I don't deal well with tight spaces and I don't try to fit into places or people that I have outgrown.
I asked for this.
I just manifested another major milestone.

Facing Truth

She serenaded me in the voice of Giveon.
She knew all I was ready to do was leave her and execute.
When I was explaining the relationship types to avoid
I was unknowingly explaining those of my own!

You need to avoid someone who disrespects you, belittles you, or harms you.
Mentally, Physically, Emotionally, Spiritually or Psychologically
They rarely started that way.
I did a mental rundown of all my relationships chronologically.
I was living life through others like a midnight rendezvous.

Trick or treat.
I smelled something sweet, and it was me.
I walked away from what was emotionally harming me, with bravery.
I am so proud of me.
I got that natural dopamine running through me.
OMG
That sizzle and the goosebumps it gave me.
Questioning *"Is what I am used to worth leaving?"*
Y
E
S
Absolutely
You better believe it!
So here I am.
Waving good-bye

Embodying and being who I truly deserve
By putting me first
I stopped settling for crumbs!
I stopped accepting bare minimums.
As if that was a trait to equate complacency.
I deserve the love that's full of the maximum.
Fulling up my cup to the brim and watching it overflow.

Food Pantry

Standing and waiting in line
I was the first so maybe I am blessed
Tears welting as I am belting.
I was scared because I had only 20 dollars in my name.
I have no one to turn to but Resources for the homeless
Who said that I would be here again?
Being alone, isolated and confused
That wasn't my plan
I cried I got hugs and prayers from strangers.
A Friar wanted to hear my story
I cried through and I screamed
Terribly
The emotional pain
This shit ain't no joke when you all alone in a place that ain't your original home
And you know no one.
A brother who for some reason in his feelings
One who can dish it but is unable to wipe his plate
He doesn't give a fuck
How many times can one hear " you're dead to me" coming from the one I called twin
I'd never do that to anyone;
I can't wrap my mind around that construct
Right now, it's fuck him
This is new to me and this one year has been a long of too many when you depend on hotels as a living
I affirm; that I am never going to be here again
I got the blessings learned lessons, and retained the value in all of them
A wave of peace overcame me while I was emotionally hysterical at the food pantry
I have no twin and we are not identical
It was a brother and I must say to him; Thank You
Tears flowed as I felt invisible but light as shit
I humbly took it and I decided to rewrite a new script

Moments

Any image through a kaleidoscope can be so beautiful and abstract.
In real life, it is like playing "*Mother May I*"
Take three steps forward and she says 'No take five steps back'!
Ashes to ashes and dust to dust
This ain't no match, not a bonus or a plus
See I know what I do not want.
I realize now what I do desire and want.
So, I align with that.

Some people I let go.
Some by default and others by choice
Too much noise so I quieted it.

I had great moments though.
That helped me heal, learn, experience, laugh, and more
Importantly grow.
Kudos to myself because I blossomed.
So much so that I capitalize on it.
The person you used to know has left.
Emerging a far better me

See every situation is a lesson!
Blessings

So, I make sure to take notes and not repeat.

Those moments I no longer go back to even though
reflections, pictures, and texts
I erased all of that.
I know myself.

Every evidence of you I deleted.
Never again will I allow a moment or person to direct me into a
Direction that's not a fit.
See I scored a home run with a new hit.

My garden is still blooming
I feel so good knowing I did right.
Those moments whether bad or good I don't desire too undue.
I know I no longer need to hold onto or go back to.

WTF Love

I attracted those who matched
The habits from my home life
We can date people who feel familiar with our upbringing
Without even realizing it
So, I dated people who treated me like my mother used to
Until the day you recognize it, and begin to change it
I changed myself to save myself
If it's all been toxic love
Then I imagine what sacred love feels like by being a reflection of it
Therapy will offer you clarity even when you don't feel you need it
I can process it now and if it makes sense
It's taken some time to get here
I had to learn to see people for who they are and not their potential
See them now where in life mentally they are at
Accept it but do not partake
It's beautiful when you can own up to your own mistakes
Now that it's understood
I will continue to work on me
I am ready to experience now what real healthy love can do!

Leave Them

People aren't as they seem.
Putting upfronts shouting out
Showing off; having the holy ghost epiphany
Yeah: I said it
But I see the clothes that you tirelessly put on daily.
I see the wolves parading like sheep.
You can't play me!
Words don't even need to be spoken.
Honestly, they aren't required.

Be careful of the wolves dressed in fashion trying to fit into your space.
As you begin to shift, they will feel stagnant.
They like a clot,
thrombase.
Their ways errant
Go ghost-like my padre.
I set the mood from the space I create and I move on easily like my vertebras.
I ain't watching no one when the action and body language says everything it needs to.

Not Another Night of This

It's nighttime and she has been dreading it all day.
Her money won't stretch a single-night stay
Savings she went through on rooms and she is trying to wrap her head around it
Circles; thoughts come out like circus clowns
Many she doesn't entertain but in the Divine, she says "I trust"
She said progression but at that moment was wondering if was it a regression
However, she thought you don't have progress if you slide back
Finding understanding in a new situation
Her kids get snuggled up in the backseat.
She is in the front diver seat
Tears now she no longer has inside
This is her first time and she searching for clarity
Her prayers were sent, and she wondered if they had been heard
Still, she didn't get a word
She got helpful friends to help get her a room
But, It's the weekend in California and they have party prices for a single night
She ensures their comfort over hers
Oh, how sweet a child to offer their comforter and warmth so mommy can be warm
Turning the engine on in the parking lot of an expensive hotel
She can say she has been there but never in
At this point in conversation….she says to herself *who fucking cares*
Watching the gas tank mileage just because the heat blowing
Her shelter is her vehicle for tonight.
Still so grateful
Ignition off
Thoughts and talks about sending her kids away because with her she felt they couldn't stay
Talks to spirit because she feels alone
No friends, no family, or a permanent home
Hotels have been their living for 4 months out of a year
Divine Blessings
She got a room the next day, showered and slept

I read something once and it said

"Surviving wartimes and war zones and coming out of them makes you a warrior"

To her kids, she is mom, to her she is trying to stay afloat
A warrior however at times gets exhausted
I wonder if she ever feels like one

Foot Prints

I walked the path and I saw footprints
Not mine
So, I am being carried by a blue gentle giant
I ain't fighting
I walked many miles with you
Then I realized that everything is better with a solid crew
This will be the new bond
It feels so damn good when you have other people speaking life into you
On the days when it was silence, only I could keep up just enough
but you spoke and sang in my ear to let me know you were there
Solid people are the only ones allowed in here

Emotional

Heavy the load with the world on my shoulders
So, I loosen my bra straps.
Nah…. I take it off and let the girls hang free.
At home got them in the mirror and together we danced.
In awe
Ask my opponents about me!
They'll say, "*We can't knock her out or down.*"
I am so focused on making myself so much better that even the critics won't argue.
I stay focused and clear.
I used to be in pain, discomfort, and disappointment and now I radiate happiness, joy, and growth.
I am here.
I am present in every moment.
Shout out to the pain that helped me acknowledge and feel my value!
Analyzing my moves and seeing a preview
Looking down from a bird's eye view
I had to wash my hands thoroughly to remove all residue.
Now, I am embracing the new
The stage lights are bright.
Confident I got this.
I have been preparing for this moment.
Breathing life into someone is way more fun.
Way more fun than my previous drug runs
Fun like trips to the gym
Defining me like an acronym
I used to send hints to go into the Tetrahedral
Get precise and loaded like a sniper with a desert eagle!
Prisons don't hold me when I already
Possess the only key!

Lighting flames on the wettest of planes
I have to admit.
To protect my energy, I will refrain.
To describe the feeling immensely.
I at times get quiet for the sake of my sanity.
Here I am telling another story, baring my soul.
No apologies: this is pure emotional

Worth

You asked me "*What is your value?*"
Well, allow me to enlighten you and give you a brief overview.
It is loving up on myself because I taste so damn delicious.
No possession just an experience
Enjoying my magnificence and embracing my significance
I took my struggles and wrapped them up into epiphanies.
I give back to whoever is listening.
Because if I allow it to stumble on me instead of mold me then
chuck it up to my faults
Open wounds don't need salt, they need healing.
So, we can chop this up over a vegan course.
I will introduce you to my source.
Take you to levels to expose your force!
Remain revolutionary but still evolutionary.
The concept is quite extraordinary.
My worth is soul-enhancing.
Helping you understand the nature of your affliction.
Which is right now about my value and what it is not giving you.
The 'NO' to panty actions.
For me, it is knowing I am a leader
There's no inferior when I am the superior.
My worth cannot be copyrighted or trademarked.
They say my bite is worse than my remarks.
Agreed!
Return to sender who doesn't want to postmark.
Highlight my thoughts and the words I say.
My value cannot be brought.
My worth…
my worth is priceless!

Trilingual

I may not know my native tongue.
But I still speak four languages fluently.
English, Spanish, you got me fucked up, and Spirit.
It moves me and grooves me.
Soothes me.
Motivates me and calms me.
It's these four languages that'll cut you down several sizes.
Gut you maliciously without any acts of violence!
You can try whomever you play, pray, or talk to
It's wise not to try me.
You may be a Trigger ...... so don't try us!
This is the first and last time this I will discuss!

I Choose Me

I know far too well the experience of being beaten down verbally.
Exhausted emotionally and mentally broken.
I mean where does it end?
It ends here with me!
First, I learned to love myself so damn hard that no critic, family member, friend, or
a lover can tear me down.
"You're stupid, shut the fuck up, retarded, I hate you, I wish I never birthed you, Bitch, I hope you die of AIDS!"
Oh yes, I heard them all and more!
They tear remnants on an etched face that is truly perplexed.
"What did I do for you to treat me this way?"
So, I chose partners based on those toxic attributes.
Well, no damn more!
Now, into myself, I pour
Giving myself more time for self-care
No more choosing myself second or last and I wondered why I was always second and last.
The sex could be good, but I'd rather masturbate.
No, we not gonna mix these energies.
I will not recreate the past; so, let me elaborate.
A must is a solid foundation that'll outlast us both.
I am more joyful, desired, loved, and happy with myself first.
Now, when my physical body meets the physical her.
She will look at me with a knowing and speak.
"Damn, I have been evolving, growing, learning, and aligning for you."
I can easily look at her and say with confidence.
"Yeah…me too"
Learning self-love is ugly.
but also, so beautiful

Journal Entry - August 2019

I have gone through periods where I wondered if I was good enough to be loved!
I desire to be loved. To be accepted for who I am and how I am.

I question if settling is just enough for me. It's not.
When I settle; things around me are built on co-dependency,
Inconsistency, unhealthy habits, and unhappiness.
That's what it is now.

I had expectations of others and none for myself. I didn't show up for it. I had looked for me in others who at times rejected me. Just looking for the love growing up that I never received

I am asking others to give me what I didn't possess or feel within myself once: Confidence, stability, security, beauty, commitment, Acceptance and a loving family.

The pictures don't tell the truth. I had only known fear, sadness, abuse, and unhappiness and that's what I received. I desire different and the only one who can give me that is me!

So, I embrace who I am and how I am now.
I see beauty within me, and I begin to embrace the mirror.
This is my new love!
Instead of critiquing myself, I have been uplifting myself through words!
A New Power for me!

Don't Box Me

I am so much more than the words I speak.
The crowds I move to and the language I am.
I am not just a poet, but an artist, an entertainer, an entrepreneur, an author, a writer, and a mother.
I am the creator.
I am a healer with my thoughts, womb, words, and my presence with the light I carry.
I know I am meant to shine.
Today I may draw figures but
I can paint a portrait tomorrow.
I am an artist in every sense and every capacity.
I am so much more; a few words still won't define me.
I am ample.
I am growing constantly.
Labels don't label or define me.
I desire so much more.
I love to see what these wings of mine are about to do

Do not allow a label to hinder you because they ultimately only box you!

Pride

You said my pride has always gotten in my way.

You were right!

It was my pride that said,

Hold on, don't give up, and give her some time, what is it gonna look like
Wait it out and stay.

I wouldn't let me leave you.

Until that day!

My child and I matter and in that, there's never a downplay!

I Let Go

last night in a space you never occupied.
Understandably, you were so familiar.
I woke up waiting for you to walk through the door.
What was I waiting for?
I was assured I would let you go.
I had got rid of all remnants, pictures, and gifts.
Pawn shops, donations, or the trash
Except the one that meant the most
The one that to me.... held the most value.
I pardoned with the gift that you said enhanced my beauty.
You picked them out.
On my ears, they sparkled, and I remembered.
To get what I truly deserve
I had to let you go entirely.
All this for a pair of earrings?
The lessons, yea!
I talked to them like I used to talk to you.
Except this time, I was direct.
I shed tears and became exhausted but filled.
With the emotions, I got so raw and real
I had love, hatred, and then peace.
I got so filled with real happy emotions that were so foreign.
That's when I knew I won.
If it tied me to you, I took action
I got rid of everything acidic and only ingested alkaline.

Cougar

I settled for pieces of you.
Especially the ones that were broken
Distorted and ragged edges that didn't mend well with my glue.
I guess that's why I felt I lucked up when I met you.
Don't eat shattered or broken glass.
No circus actor acrobat
I took your pieces and made them digestible into a fine grain.
I ate every word and punch whether physical or not.
I sprinkled it on everything.
Now I understand why I got injured.
Physically and emotionally within you searching for a foundation.
Only hoping every step didn't cause your trigger.
We were walking on eggshells in my home.
It was never you.
You were the fun inner child I never knew and the laughter I never had.
However, your anger I could not comprehend,
a loose cannon,
A woman off her meds and on a loose hinge
What's the definition of insanity?
At one time you could point it towards me!
I was looking for love externally
When all I had to do was look internally
Heal her and get acquainted so that I can say I know every part of her.
People ask why I smile so much now.
I say it started when I took control of my mind, and it got sharper and wiser.

February 2014

Karma

Mirror, Mirror on the wall you finally reveal yourself to me
Ever saw yourself within someone else
It's not you but they are doing everything you used to do.
Yeah, I'm talking to you.
Serving facts
Alerting to who I used to be.
So, I sympathize with it.
Told on myself and didn't honor my code.
It's the price you pay when you go down this road.
I faced issues and truths you wanted me to forget.
However, the lessons had to be felt and then told.
My triggers were from people and environments that imitated
whatever inside I was feeling, and it was projected back to me!
It's what I attracted.
What I had to see to gut it out
I am gifted and bold.
The shattered pieces
Sharp edges of people and situations had me remold.
That's how it is.
You can't face the facts if you can't acknowledge your own.
reflections
Karma; now is importance of mastering.
another lesson

Fact checks: - anything you do will always at some point in life be reflected to you at some point– remember that

Real One

I am perfection with flaws
I embrace not disgrace things I may still be feeling
I know I am worth it.
The glow on your face
The meat on your sandwich
The sweets since you into treats
The speaker in your voice box
I am built like the pyramids.
Secret chambers only exposed to a few.
Some knowledge is hidden but revealed when it's fitting.
I am of value.
Like the value of a black diamond; rare
Not calculated
I do things differently.
I am the goof that also uplifts you with my serenades of whatever
song pops into my mind.
Let's keep the convo going randomly by just talking.
Let's think outside the box
I want whatever we do for the memory to stay
I am a real one.

Step In and Step Out

When others were stepping out you stepped in
Offering by verbalizing your heart
Then the excitement settled.
I watched your actions and your words.
Nothing was aligning.
Rebuilding; is the beginning of my new start.
I didn't realize that you too were just like my previous.
So, I serve up a salute to you because that's what's best.
I used to assume that those around you would also hold you down.
Then I realized that not everybody is on team Qui
Damn, these seasonal folks I called friends; I held onto them too long,
but they helped me though!
Helped me to craft my present and shape my future.
They stepped in momentarily.
Giving with a veil of true and false intentions
Your alibi does not fit the reflections you show.

What's real is I got those tears out and released the sorrow that
followed.
You stepped in for your gain.
It could have also been genuine under the circumstances.
Thank you for being the raft I needed.
However, I stepped out.
More lessons and purges
Hidden are my whereabouts.
I outgrew the *"used to and the frequently."*
The time came when I have removed myself.
Indefinitely

Clear

I said I would write about you until I have nothing else to say.

Until there is no more feeling
I put so much faith in you.
I wanted to carry your last name.
I wanted to birth your family.

Then I got it all out

Well

I have no words left to say.

I am clear.

Cry for You

I stopped shedding tears on the things and people I could not change.

Some things are meant to change, and others are to stay the same.
My place in it does not remain.
So
I'll send you a Hallelujah if that's what you used to
Ase, Ase, Ase, O
So, I plant my seeds and fulfill my needs.
Then come back to you.
I put you in that box of Pandora.
I am giving it back to you.
May whoever opens the contents of you be ready for a surprise!
The magnitude that you bring does not subside.
Maybe through time!
I do not care

I am no longer looking in the rearview

I no longer cry for you.

Me

I got lost.
I knew my body was being lifted.
I gave in
I got lost in the recovery.
My body was found floating senselessly among the debris.

Who is going to love me?
Tell me "You're beautiful"!
Who is going to love me like this?

She came forward and said I do!
There I stood talking and acknowledging me.

Her Story

My first confession was with a straight razor to my artery in the
bathroom to my carotid at age thirteen doing what I saw on TV
I was scared it was going to hurt.
It was one thing to inflict harm on another but fuck; not to myself.
I consider that a blessing.
I'm not concerned with what people will say.
Ain't none ever try to walk in these shoes.
Many don't want to
So why should I care?
Lifelong dreams that manifest
Got me painted like the Kemetic Queens inside the
Ancient Egyptian Pyramids
I'm on the walls painted in Hieroglyphics.
What can I say, I am no hybrid!
Do you want to hear my side, the truth, or a lie?
Truth, is I don't have it all together; who does?
I am still trying to understand this crazy ass weather.
The truth is some people are of shadows the past.
Others can be imprinted.
Now I just walk the path designed just for me.
I have got a sharp tongue, I wear what makes me feel good, At times
I rock Ankh earrings.
I now carry my sign that says.
"I am a TEN."
I fell back in love with my pen.
Named her "*Just Right*" and we make love in ink.
We gave birth to a seed and I call her *ART*.
She is my other heart.
So, I paint it, sing it, write it how I think.
They said it's me creating.
I am dressed for a feast.
Some will call me a beast.
However, there's a slight problem.
This beauty is unlike a beast because I don't eat meat!

Move On

How do you?

M
O
V
E

Like that
I picked solitude, healing, presence, and clarity.
I watched you get ready for some new ass.
We all cope and deal differently.
What is a new start?
How do I know I did exactly right?
Well, I learned to love myself and to embrace every ounce of me.

How do you move on?

With a clear mind, an abundance of space for the right one
Clearing out what comes with sad tears knowing that there is
something and someone so much better than this.

Spaces that take me places; a heart that continues to grow.

This is my testimony.

Resilience

How many failures?
How many S…K…C…A…B…T…E…S
Setbacks
How many
T
E
A
R
S

Before there is a win
Do you know how it feels to be left in the wind?
It beats on your face.
Do you know how high you can go when you are weightless?
Without indecisiveness, without regret holding you back.
How resilient are you?
Doing what no one believed I could do.
Doing what I love to do.
Resilience laid exactly right, paired with long natural lashes, a perfect lippie and the strong confidence to match.
They might have brought fire, fuel, and ammunition but you cannot take down this bridge that you didn't help to build.
I am the blueprint with the fine print
Speaking in tongue, lip-locking with a positive life-like
With her, I will go wherever she goes
I cherish her.
A I M
The best women come with the game,
From life experiences.
I guess that makes me…… qualified.
I name this one resilience.

Can I Lay With You?

Can I lay my head on your chest and listen to you with each breath you take?
I want to feel your heartbeat; Let it sync with mine and develop its link.
Watching the rise and fall of your chest.
Can I lay in your arms and feel the safety and security?
that I find pleasure?
Can I fall asleep to your heartbeat?
The thumping of this complex and unexplored mechanism that fuels your body, allows me to quietly pleasure in its dynamic
Damn, I love it!
I love to lay on your body and watch the very curves of your nature as it entices me to seductively pleasure you with my thoughts.
I want to taste the sweetness of caramel with the saltiness of sweat.
I want to feel that throb on the tip of my moist peak that drips seasons.
I want to feel the air quality change from that mountain climb.
It's like Mount Everest and with it we defeat.
It can get cold, but together we generate more than enough heat.
Let us melt like snow!
Can I stroke your hair as you whisper your dreams into the air?
Admiration for such an exquisite and extraordinary being.
Your Genuity.
Iwa Pele
Excuse me if I don't refrain from my thoughts.
Is it inappropriate that I just want to fondle your heart and reassure you that I have loved it and you from the start?
Way before I knew you!
I feel and I am worthy enough of your dialect.
that speaks to me in a language that only you can speak.
And I comprehend.

Can we sit and enjoy this view of the sunset?
Nothing too complex.
The vision is love that sees equally.
The best picture from memory that can ever be framed beautifully.

I want to be your canvas.
Paint me with your intelligence and love!
Know that I am your support in more ways than one!
Wrap and cover me with your blanket of thoughts and laughter!
Let's speak out and talk about our goals, visions, ambitions, and dreams.
I want the warmth from all that we desire.
Only one thing is required.
Can I just lie with you?

Unpack

I have boxes that I have opened but I want to know,
Can I unpack within you?
It's not baggage unless it's bags we pack together.
It's every drop of indulgence I got for you.
Every breath inside of me.
I want to breathe into this.
I'm delicate but not fragile.
I'm tough but still sensual.
I'm rough but still possess a soft touch.

I am not just trying to unwrap for the show and see where we go.
I'm saying let's lay a strong foundation, and have a few babies.
Be committed because I am with it.
Stay sober on life and all she possesses.
Love like our own movie
Directed, produced, and unedited by us.
Let's polish shit!
Like real wood, rims, granite tiles, and car seats that we going to lay in and get in
And our hearts
They glow and together they're blinding.
I want to be on all your sides.
Because I am part of our anchor
Your woman; your foundation; your home
We know its alignment because we feel it.
Allow these energies to meet, greet, and ***make love before*** *we do!*
So, I am saying,

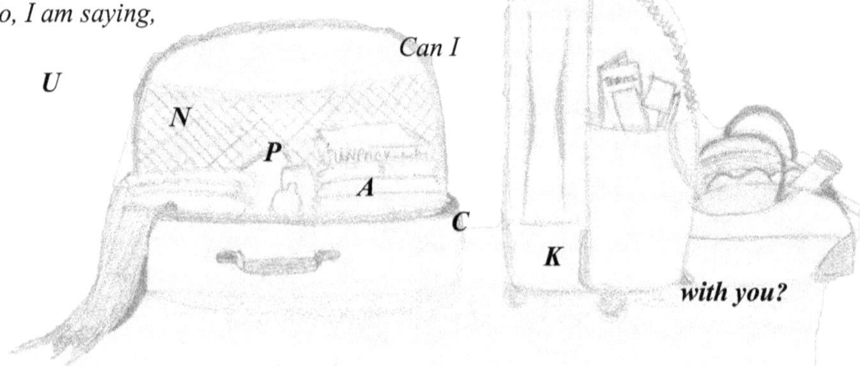

Can I

U
N
P
A
C
K

with you?

I affirm that when I unpack.

Physically
Mentally
Intellectually
Emotionally
Spiritually
and
Any other attribute that is required and desired.

It will be gifted, blessed, aligned, and manifested Spiritually with divinity!

October 2019

Feminine Energy

The skies are wide open, and they call and sing to me.
It's kind of unique to explain.
It's not recorded, hasn't been written, and at times not even verbalized.
I feel calm, I have peace.
Our revolution will be televised.
That is the divine feminine energy.
It's feeling, sensing, hearing words spoken, and knowing for a fact.
It's also the signs that only I see.
The production rains within me.
Together our songs are beautiful and I'm sure yours are too.
It breathes life into me and those that I am close to
Soothes and heals my wounds; with her waters, I am renewed.
Says "You will continuously grow".
Know your place is high and use your voice every day.
Oh, she can serenade me into anything.
Positively impacts people that stay planted but ready.
The melodies she sings to me say get up and do everything.
that you stand for and stand against
Forget the rest of the distractions of nonsense!
When the Universe is my stage and my beat
Let the fingers and the sounds groove you!
Like a Beyoncé song do
Like Nipsey Hussle, Kendrick Lamar, Tupac Shakur, Rapsody,
Chronixx, Koffee, or Nas song that inspires you.
Lay those bricks and let the pipe bombs of knowledge tick and
explode
Tattoo tongues
Create and decorate the place that you have become!
This is for everyone.
Reclaiming your Queendom.
The womb space is the Feminine divine energy

Gratitude

Without you, I can fall short of my excavations
Slow, fast, giving, and mind-blowing.
Show gratitude.
I show you appreciation.
You always know exactly what to do to make me call on you.
Yea, you are exactly right.
Feeling so good on my skin next to you
Thank You
For every relationship, a moment I took for granted, every milestone, every prison call accepted, every violent act I escaped or committed.
Every day: I breathe in you.
Yeah, I am showing my gratitude.
You put me in the mood.
Candlelight's with rose petals and Moscato
It's just me tonight!
More than enough, great substance mixed with sweet juices of appreciation that is forceless with a pinch of richness
Like on those blunts that I like to hit now and again!
Gratitude, I love you.
Thank You
Bless Up
I express it daily.
I just wanted to share what mine looks and feels like

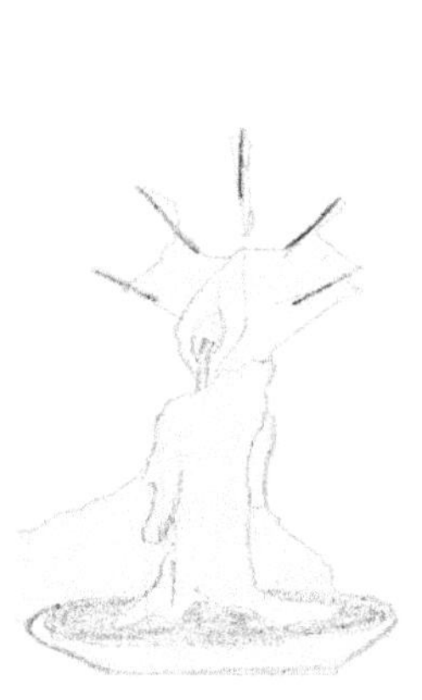

Four Play

Kiss me softly and caress my intelligence.
Finger it and watch her burst into deep conversations.
Talking about spiritual worlds, saving animals, and loving everyone.
Penetrate slowly and deeply and hear her moan as you stroke her
thoughts sharing accumulated knowledge!
These deep conversations feel much like sex.
Gaze into her eyes and see galaxies that are unknown to so many.
She said it felt good to be gripped from behind, hair pulled and
exposing every thought, she spoke
Every vision she affirmed and every moment she manifested.
This intense lovemaking is beautiful.
Glorifying what I call sex.
This is my kind of foreplay

I am an intellectual person.
I am an Aquarius.
Deep conversations are so gratifying and appealing to me.

There is something about going into a deep conversation with the person and/or people that you are with!

The deeper the conversation the deeper the connection I make.

A partnership isn't all sexual!
That's the physical
Outside of great sex, what else is there?

There must be a real connection with my mental

Penetration on a soul and intelligence level.

What books have you read and can talk to me about them? Break it down and I will still read for my interpretation.
What knowledge can we share and learn from one another?

A solid foundation to me starts with the intellect!
I want to learn, grow, teach, be taught, and elevate.
My opinion

The New

I walked out on you.
For a cross-country road trip to a new destination
I turned and left without any type of sigh.
Just relief
I'll make my pen do what I can no longer do.
Cry for you
Tears have been shed; just no longer with me.
Not even internal
Clarification gave me constant motivation.
No justification is needed.
I was over being told that,
"The one who needs to change is, you!"
When the entire household did therapy except for you
Name-calling and shaming me in front and behind me.
I am too educated for the low vibratory.
You know what happens to a woman when she is at her peak?
She detaches without a break and leaves with a clean slate.
My heart ain't hurting it's beating to the tune of life.
Leaving is so freeing, and so therapeutic.
I have fresh ears listening to new music.
I obtained a clear mental.
I find myself incredibly attractive and very appealing!
I don't know **what the FUCK** you were thinking.
I take fault; we never had synergy.
Facts.
I left our lie of a life in your hands while we played Jeopardy.
I learned to brew strong energy.
Focused and poured it back into me.
Been too long but it's finally here.
Everything is positively stable and brand new.

Forbidden Fruit

They say don't take more than what's needed.
However, I tasted more than my palate could decipher, and you did too.
Picking you, devouring you, and indulging
right on time
Juices mixed, smoothies blended, and we ascended.
You say the peach is sweet.
I know it's just as sweet and juicy as can be.
Devour this, devour me, and let me devour you!
That is what you asked!
Slippery, delectable, indulgence, an entrée
Encore
There is room for more.
You tasted my fruit and got my juices all over you.
This fruit was only forbidden until it ripened.
So, peel me like a mango using your tongue and teeth.
Savor me like your favorite sweet treat!
I want to be sound asleep.
In your arms
As we lay in our bed where we are creating and planting seeds
We doubleheader, full on our missions and a means.
Lick your fingers, drink the juices
This is the kind of chemistry we
Produce!

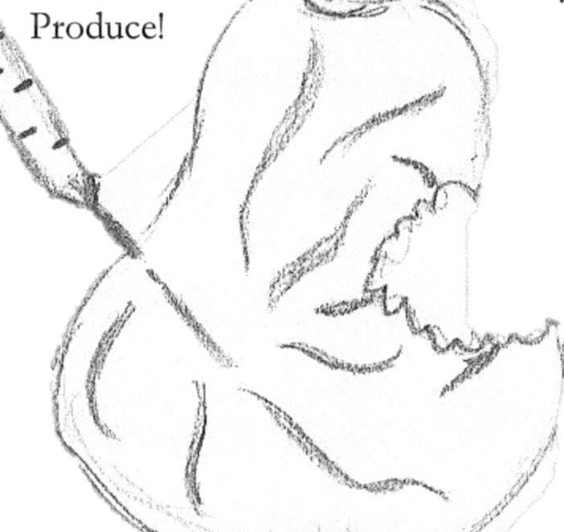

We're Open

I can smell your scent.
You feel like a sanctuary.
To this Aquarius born in February
That's a deep feeling.
They say we don't feel much.
But with you, I feel all five senses of your touch
You are spacious, inviting, loving, sexy, intellectual, funny, and peaceful.
The openness in your arms opened wide.
Full of the openness I have been guided to
You got it feeling like summer.
Quenching thirst like a hot and dry day
I am ready to come out and play.
You are my shelter.
My day and night light
You
Are
Better
I got new sheets and new pillows where our heads will go.
Everything is brand new.
We are now home.
Come on in, I have been expecting you!

Here are to wide open spaces.

Seat at my Table

Who we invite makes all the difference.
Plates on the table and we eat off each other's opinion.
Break bread with our ideas
Like it is communion
Baked right like a homemade biscuit.
Adding ingredients
Like good thinking and putting our minds together
Brainstorming on new endeavors
This is what I am talking about.
We are stable.

I Got You

I intend to show you.
It has always been on the strength of you and what we have been through.
You deserve the best and the finest.
In my Queendom you are my Royal Highness
I invested in you.
Although I am still learning
Confident that this all happened for a reason.
Baby girl we are driving to the new season.
All I ever want for you is to be happy.
I know that resides with family.
The best part about all of this is that we got that and more.
I needed to say that out loud.
We are so good.
My priceless gem
The abundance that is here and now
The blessings are for us.
I am focused.
It's Epic and beautiful.
I am so grateful that the one person I get to experience and enjoy all this with is you!
Getting all, you want and desire because you deserve it.
Together we are building.
This is the best feeling.
You do live up to your name.
You are *my favorite love.*

Mi Nina Bonita

Me

A silhouette of what love is.

Seeping out of my maple sap bearing fruit free

Eating the nectar of your fruition

Ripened to perfection by seasons of change.

From the gardening of growth and personal reflections

I love you.

Chosen

Oooh, Look at you.
Unlimited potential
Boss lady
CEO
Owner
Enlightened one,
shining,
giving energy
Loving life,
living life,
being a vessel
Showing no limits
Being positive, giving light
Giving love
Life feels so good!
Helping people along the way
Leaving lights on, tied ropes, a way, a path unlike none known.

You are chosen.

Ooouuu, You Killing It

I Put in the time and reflect.
This is what I want, I aspire to be so this can go.
Anywhere I flow.
Taking risks
This feels like Big Shit.
Moving and shifting out
New avenues, there's more to you.
So, I make time for myself.
I love up on her, make love to her.
Whispering in her ear like damn you're fine.
I am gonna love you for life like Jodeci.
You the shit!
Or, you are killing it.
Go girl!
Ooouuu, you got this
You work hard and go through.
So, this is for you.
Gassing myself up
That's a lion walking.
That's a tiger walking.
I am a Panther.
Yeah, I am stepping out on this.
The Empress emerged.
I am right on time.

Becoming Forever

When I catch feelings it's a different organic.
Specific
Like the strings on an acoustic
Delicate
Architectural means and I supply my desires.
Do you know there are various expressions of love?
So, I express mine poetically.
It is the
Fall on me if you have to!
Count on me like you do digits.
Love me, want me, want us.
Crave my thoughts and sentiments!
I'll share with you all of her brilliance.
Piece by piece
I'll reveal to you the beautiful expression.
My foundation is solid mentally.
I have a home that speaks to my stability.
I Planted seeds that came to bear fruit and roots physically.
I am her forever.

Riding Smooth

It is like a high
And I got sky miles.
I keep my crown pointed to the sky.
I went from living in hotels and straight to flying on clarity.
I paddled treacherous seas and eventually, it was just me.
I landed, got warm, with eyes on home and lots of palm trees.
I did this all with initially my mini me on day one.
Guidance from the spirit and the ancestral realms
My rider
Actions are facts if we are speaking about that.
Sometimes it rained and it became muddy, but I was gifted with intuition and clarity.
I was nervous but I knew we'd be good.
I had dirty nails from funneling myself out.
It allowed me to slide away.
I give thanks to Olodumare, the Most High, and the mothers.
You the Blessings.
The lessons
Gave me gem souvenirs.
I am overflowed with the wonders of my brand-new surroundings.
So, the smoke you see is just from the tires screeched.
I go from Eric Bellinger, Koffee, Sampha the Great, Rapsody, Buju Banton, Nipsey Hussle, Etana, and more all in one day.
Now you know a little more about me.
I am grounded.
I am happy.
I am balanced.
I am abundant.
I am on a strong foundation with deep roots.
It feels so good to say that now we are riding smoothly.

Going Forward

PTSD and traumas no longer capture me.
I am not afraid.
I am greater than anything.
Greater than the dark that used to try me.
Oh, they wanted to reappear!
They used to taunt and test by asking.
"Will you come to play with me?"
Bitch, get off me because I am determined and focused.
They wanted this Goddess riddled with fear.
How do you retrain a mind that has been conditioned?
You relearn to depend on your intuition!
Like I just knew and heard without knowing the facts.
I felt it!
Now you know why I can be distant.
Why do I go hard and stay persistent?
It is your energy coming for mine that ain't mixing.
I am not boasting or high-strung.
I can give you a good lashing using only my triple tongue.
I cleared out space.
I leave behind, sell, or give away what can be better replaced.
I am going forward.
Positive attention I garnered.
I moved to a warmer zip code.
The Blessings are coming in by the truckloads.

Ase

Catch

I recall chats about this very,
Moment!
Having a blast even though at the time it hadn't happened yet!
Worry used to set in on my face.
I used to sit and wait for you.
Wanted you to feed me intimacy.
I knew you couldn't, so I fed myself.
I got smart and got in my boat ready to sail.
I wasn't going to miss the tide.
 I am ready to enjoy this ride.
I am stronger.
Became Mr. T because I meant nothing was stopping me.
I am a good woman.
And we don't stay in the market long.

I am the greatest catch.

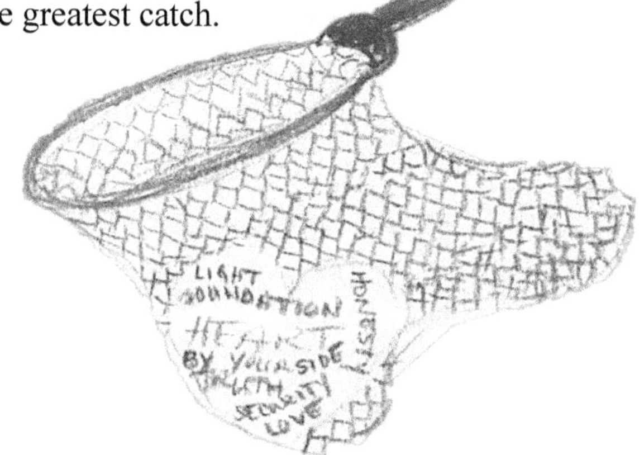

New Faces

History doesn't mean we stay together.
It doesn't mean people don't change.
We all know they do.
Everyone should want to
It implies that a historical moment has been made.
Like knowing that at times a new experience can only happen with someone else.
Somewhere new
Our history has traveled some miles and years and picked up a few laughter's, and cheers.
I don't why I didn't see it.
That the only person I needed to remove was me

I have no apologies.

2019 / 2020

Peace in Anxiety!

You can never possess people; only experience them.
So, allow me to experience you.
Your highs and your lows
I can be a tissue and your pillow.
Your laughter and your happiness
Your joy and your peace
Especially your smile
With one another we can be vulnerable.

Let me be a part of the reason you smile but not the only reason!
Shit let me experience every aspect of you.
Your story and what you have been through.
However,
Never do I want to possess you.

For Me

Love me to infinity!
Grab me like YOU ARE GRASPING the wheel to the new two-seater!
Get excitement written all over your face when you see me.
Read me, sing me, Capture and feel me.
Energetically we can be connected.
I express my gratitude to the most high for you.
I swear in your presence there is always calm.
Together we are changing the bloodline genome.
I get lead foot when I am ready to come home.
Red lights I run just to get to get to you.
Yea, wine, bubbles, and dinner sounds sexy.
We have been waiting for this.
You show off your true flex.
I am in a way new mental and physical space.
You said, *"Just be safe I've waited a lifetime for you."*
You are more than what I asked for.
I'm on the way.
To our sacred place

This is What It Feels Like

The thrill of seeing you.
I am Feeling you Finally.
It still Sends my body deep electrical waves.
Got me doing cartwheels for days.
Hand splits, and active movements with my body and I am rejoicing.
While you are whispering and nibbling my name.
The warmth of your foundation is stillness and I reside at our permanent address.
Walking within your walls ensures safety.
My feet tickle your carpet, and it feels so good that I lay my head on it.
You fill me up with surprises.
Amazing
With you every day, we are up in sync.
Together watching and gazing at all the sunrises.
At night we watch the sunset
While sipping on wine or smoking a Jay
This forever is every day.
You place your stance and say this is where we permanently lay.
Our smile is surreal because you are real.
When the moon blesses us
She does so with flow.
I kiss every one of your freckles.
Others call them stars.
You're the pot of gold within the rainbow.
We lay every night under her because she feels so good.
Especially with you!
Curving and outlining our silhouettes.
The perfect angle; no contour or shading
It's wet.
From a rain downpour

But outside we stay and lay.
Enjoying these drops, sprinkled and tickled when separately we both experienced droughts.
Brief bouts where the ground was a little shaky.
It's super solid now though.
Strong roots too
I love to hear from you every day.
The sounds are seasoned.
Our imperfections are beauty marks that we perfected.
You delight me, recite, you know me.
The way you hold my scent and the way I carry yours
A new legacy for my family.
It's been far too long.
We are here now where we both agree.
I tell her daily Thank You and that I am grateful.
She is my HOME and MY TREE!

The Driver Seat

I research and understand a broken thesis.
Broken down and so poetically spoken.
It's a blessing that together we get to read them.
Come float in my mother ocean.
Pollinate my flowers.
Water my roots
Coconut oil my body for your field
You scored a touchdown.
Free throw
For real
I am your cipher.
The dialect you used to search for but now I am at your fingertips.
Your fingerprints are imprinted with my DNA.
By design
You didn't have to high-speed chase me.
GTA
No backtracks.
No look-backs.
I mean that.
You wanna vex.
Let me hear about it.
Go meditate.
I have a place that has the space for you to get that.
Gravity
Lifting your chin, kissing your forehead.
Intentionally infusing you with affirmations
Listening internally
We give cheers to all our dope conversations
There are plenty.
We love the sand in between our toes.
We solidify with ratios while smoking the tree and keeping the score of Uno.
Hop in today I am driving.
anywhere
Let's go!

Full Moon in Cancer

December 31, 2020

I read your borders to kiss you that night.
At least by sunset
I maneuvered your walls and paved the cement.
I found resistance.
I said I had it until
You decelerated into another open space and there I was in unfamiliar terrain
With kids
Yet you would not let me go.
So, I could only proceed.
Gas petal delayed traction.
Foot reactions
But I still choose to trust you.
So, to not panic I just cruised and then I saw you.
I saw you behind the night clouds.
Still illuminating the night sky
I called you forward.
Full moon in Cancer
Blessing my face with your glory
You parted your clouds, waved the darkness away and it was just you and I in the night sky.
Traffic thick
Uncertainty within wondering if I could handle it.
Til you said, "Here in the left lane you need to stay, and you'll be safe."
This is what they call a saving grace.
Because stopping and braking with spasticity
With my unpredictable foot was dangerous enough
The traffic parted and I was cleared to go.
You kept me gazing at your beauty.
Feminine energy is the rescue.
Despite the terrain, I drove thru
I made it safely.
Brought in the new year feeling amazing.
I brought in the new year dancing to you and with you.
What happens in Vegas does not stay there.
I wear the badge of courage.

Because it reminds me of my freedom
I wear the badge of honor.
It showed me who I can truly trust.
The badge of resilience
Except this time before I cross the finish line
I call in all the lineage and Spirits.
My ancestral Army

Inside of Me

I want to
Inject you into my system.
Let you flow through my veins like an addiction.
Let your light be a rehab of submission.
I wanna……
Swim in your waters of meditation
Your golden
This has been a premonition.
Well planned out by the most high
Olodumare
You glisten within that gem called a diamond.
That makes my mantra the "OM."
To your Tibetan Bowl
Let us sit, talk, chill, and laugh for hours talking about life, love, and our passions.
Everything
Including the 7 African Powers
Sieta Las Potencias
For real
This is how it feels when you whisper in my ear.
"I wanna be inside you."

Light Work

Let my verbal satisfaction match my
physical actions and attraction.
The *"this is that frequency."*
Another level let's call it what it is.
Dope Energy
The blemishes you bear from the past.
dimensions.
Your face reflects chemistry.
Although it is a language and formula I
Understand
I still wanna overstand you and let the light
in
When we go deeper, we re-do history.
Your Periodic Table is real.
Edible and delectable
Insatiable Palate
Like a cherry full of sweet natural juices
When you bite into it will squirt
This is what we call Light Work.

Blessings

I won't fake it.
I initially didn't think I'd make it.
However, there was nothing to go back to.
I knew I would make it when I let go!
I was at first uncertain that these shots wouldn't transmit.
I dreamed, manifested, put in that work and I submitted to it.
Praise to the Most High
for this position
I said when I got here, I would always send my blessings.
There had been premonitions; and dreams spoken.
Instilled within me that now I know for sure the meanings.
They just came to me in pieces.
Before it became clear
It was a must that I surrender with faith and trust.
It's not always easy but through it all I cried and pushed.
Like a baby on its first-born day
Breathe
Fuck It; I almost several times gave up.
However, I kept picking it back up.
I let toxic people go and forgave them sincerely.
If it's costing me my peace.
I don't receive it; I will just leave it.
Walking the road alone isn't easy
There have been many nights I cried asking for an answer.
Approached by many I curved and smoking weed was my
pleasure until it was no longer appealing.
Smoke, sleep, and repeat that ain't me.
Sativa me!
I am still ascending.
Weights are lifted.
I am shifting.
In different gears
I can maneuver and glide in cars and handle the manuals.
From the first to fifth gears with ease
I take off.

The wind blows.
I am in gear mode.
GO
Let the smoke flow, collect, and settle a bit.
The tires do circles across the pavement.
I pushed off the clutch and I let go.

I know.
You prayed for my downfall.
How is that working out for you?
I take the hate, make it my bait and now I'm eating expensive vegan steaks.
Portobello
Tan outside under the father of the glowing yellow sun
The ride is meant for one but built to carry two.
Got my hija buckled up and in
The front space will always be made for you.
The truth

Matches of Melanin

I desire your fire to be like my favorite BIC.
No matter the breeze that moves you are so loyal to light me.
Speak to me like knowing that I reflect you.
More like you're a reflection of me.
Put respect on my name whenever you speak of me.
Without my existence, you would not be able to run laps
Meaning you wouldn't exist.
Who runs the world?
Women do
New age revolution, motivation, stand in position.
Realize who you talking to!
If not then you need to side-check yourself and come back and acknowledge that I am a woman backed with deep melanin with ancient history,
Buried secrets embedded within my DNA.
Can you feel that?
I can hold the heat.
Blast at them lyrically, physically, and mentally.
Spoken well by Malik El Hajj Shabazz
By any means necessary
My melanin spills out and pumps to you.
Remember a woman like me birthed you.
I am the WOMB man.
So, we deserve all the clout and accolades.
For all the times you mistreated.
Performing under the pedigree
When I unload all my ammunition and let the bullets fly
I am Mecca, Madam, Coretta, Betty, Auset and Assata
Backed by all the ancestors.
Bet you did not know that.
So, sit with the seat back.
Smoke a little bit and take a sip!
You got me fucked up.
My personality is legit but unique.
I been that; done that; test me and you gone meet my Nip.

Adios

Your intentions were not pure.
Let's keep it real.
Keep it a brick we both mature.
Contemplating if I should go back to the old me.
Overdosing on meditations; not really
Constellations and getting massive revelations.
I was wondering if today the day would be I get sporadic and erratic.
I worked too damn hard to get into the space of a place that used to be hard to get to
Fucked over by someone who still searching.
To take like a merchant
You cannot buy me your fake smile even when it's free.
and only in me can I invest heavily.
I was a part of the Hocus Pocus while you sucked on my energy.
Almost lost my life and sanity.
When I looked in the mirror, I was staring at a reflection of who I used to be with vanity.
Reaching for the bottle of toxicity and getting drunk off her reflection, issues, and self-hatred
I guess leeches sucking on my blood was miraculous.
You are the picture of a calamitous.
Rare types like O-negative
I tried, applied, and learned that you cannot save everyone,
They will drown you with the weights they carry.
So, they live and thrive off your energy.
So, leave and pick up the pieces.
Giving you the Peace sign-up with index down!
Conmigo todo es final
I ain't mad at ya I just don't fuck with you now.
Y eso es real

Good Love

I'm that good love.
That Trey Songz's Anticipation 1 and 2 kinda love
I got that Dexta Daps.
Kranium No Odda
Etana Proppa
I am positioning you in all kinds of love traps!
I got that Seven Streeter Sex on the Ceiling
You say that I give you that type of feeling.
I am that real H-Town, Silk, Maxwell playing.
Al. B Sure to fill up your cup with love.
James Baldwin, Patrice Lumumba, and Nikki Giovanni write a poem about you.
The "let's talk" type of love
That I got ya back, front, side, top and bottom.
Your all-sides Hexagon
The light, your energy and I promise I give off plenty.
I am the calm in your storm.
The peace in your midst
The sun in the hurricane
Like the Olokun to call back the seas
Yemoje nursing and gifting you the desires and the calms that you please.
I am with you when you experience your highs and your lows.
Within those lies your vulnerability
I am there for both!
I am a good love!
I am not perfection, but I am the enhancement of your reflections.
When they see me, they know that what I possess and embody and know it is also with you.
I keep your name relevant from the streets to the boardrooms and interviews.
Know that I got you.
I love what the elder folks tell you about.
It feels like peace.
I am the peace because it resides within me.
Have you floating in love, birth all ya babies, carry your name.
For keepsake leave a piece of me on you for safekeeping.
That fragrant aroma that stays with you when you leave.
Yea, I am that kind of love.

The sweet tooth that satisfies.
Your mouth-watering bite,
You cannot get enough kind of love.
It is refreshing knowing I am who you desire.
You dream and you call out my name in your sleep.
What I possess and offer
Is that…

I love you long time!

Ooooh Lawd it's a Fire!

I am watching you move.
I must say you're the sexiest thing I've ever seen.
The wind is blowing, and I feel the heat
The throb between my legs from watching you sway in a variety of ways,
Doing the Victory dance
your rhythm and the way you move to your beat.
Yes, I got horny starring and watching the flames of a firepit
Seriously this is real shit, lol.
The Temperature is rising.
I see flames, I feel the heat.
Raheem Devaughn ain't even on rotation yet
If I was a dude, I'd have an erection
But thank you Divine; I am who I am.
Right now is am aroused in my pants watching you do the fire dance
The marbles still are glistening
You are beautiful; even better when you lit

Don't Let Go

I was running, breathing, heaving, and under an attack.
Not any form of embellishment
This shit was resentment.
Buried in pockets deep.
Like drugs wrapped in plastic and placed in Gain liquid
Behind the seat and in disguise
The shit you can see in clear sight but still overlook.
Ain't no trade or bargaining with her because all she wanted was me.
Bloody knives in hands
Gun in the holster that she could pull out, but she liked the adrenaline for fun.
I was now on the run.
Stab wounds
Rope marks around my neck
This is what happens when you do not keep yourself in check.
I thought I was outrunning but was still hanging myself.
Repeatedly
Knocks on the door but I was only opening for those that I know.
Familiarity
I guess I did not recognize that the other person I didn't know was me.
Guess who came to dinner and she is dragging all the bodies in tow.
To high are the windows
So, I bang on them desperately looking for something or someone to rescue me.
She got closer and dragged me by my Locs.
She handcuffed me to the seats.
She was taking me on a date to the beach
It's dark and pitch
She had a clear shot; they would only hear the gunshots.
No suspect because she can get away in the dark and arrive on the scene just to watch.
And admire her work and show unfold.
Her clever work
A real Picasso.
I did the only thing I knew.
I sent a Universal text and made a call amid her pursuit.
Thank you, Apple, location!
As she begins to raise her hand
The lightning, wind, and the thunder began.
Oya and Shango

All the ancestors came down to rescue me and then they all cut her throat.
My squad got her down.
Tied her to bricks and dropped her body to the bottom of the ocean with Olokun.
I cannot explain to you all that I have been through, what was taken, and what I was given.
What I do know is to never let go
Of your belief, trust, and firm hope!

Spark Up

I'm so damn talkative.
I'm so friendly too.
Don't take this smile as submissive!
My words are still explicit.
I'm a reflection of you.
Guns I can disarm.
Heads I can chop off.
I'm full-on flight tonight
My cup overflows on sight

My smile mesmerizes and glows.
Blows up your ego.
Upgrade your mindset and thought process!
Turns up the nozzle on your intellect.

Introduce you to another version of yourself.
I will expose every gem you have hidden.
Lock away and keep your secrets.
Be your cheerleader at every achievement.
From the minute to the grand
A la pequeño o el grande
Skateboard this life with your heart on the physical, emotional, psychological, and mental levels.
Because we all need to hear that
Cual es su nivel

People are so consumed with their thoughts.
It's good to break away from the things mundane
To a person that's verbally insane
Full of knowledge that can make you pull away from reality and escape to a place that isn't hard to go.
If you understand that before you lead, at times you must follow.

No Apologies
I'm not a link-up.
At times I pass you by
Briefly and we may spark it up.

Sometimes we get a few moments of a text or a call.

No worries we can still kick it.
We gone chill and spark up and at times spark up.
On my one, two, puff and pull and pass ass.
Look at that!
I can also make you laugh.

The New Moon

I settled for pieces of you.
Especially those that were broken
Believing it was the best I could do.
Shattered pieces don't mend well with my glue.
I guess that's why I felt I lucked up when I met you.
Don't eat shattered or broken glass!
Not even upon its discovery because it'll internally kill you.
I know I am No circus actor or acrobat
But I ate every word and every punch whether physical or non.
And still, I sprinkled it on everything.

Now I am learning why I got physically restricted.
My body shut down and the dialogue that asked me to question my own space mentally.
Physically and emotionally
Being in search of a foundation
Only for it to be quicksand.
Lesson learned.

It was never in you.
Then my final act was that I honestly was waiting to use that 9 mm on myself hidden within the glove compartment.

What's that definition of insanity?
At one point you could have looked at me
Looking for love externally
When all I had to do was look internally
Heal her and become acquainted so much that I can say I am still learning and am getting to know every part of her
People ask why I smile so much.
I say it started with the new moon.

New Book of Life

This is a New book
The old chapters have been closed and a new book has been started and opened
No more dipping and dappling
In Places that place its value in toxicity.
I have been finding reasons and things to forgive myself for.
Acknowledging my internal dialogue has been way off
I was surrounded mostly by off energy whether verbal or a presence
I was overextending myself
Til I became thin
I'm saying that with either choice I give my attention to manifests.
I know this to be true because I manifested someone I thought I wanted and I realized
Nah this ain't it
So, I gave it back
Reflecting and asking "What I am fucking looking for"
Forgiving hands?
Reviewing lesson plans?
On life!
No, I am not taking bullshit just the fact that I desire something different
I know what it feels like to not be wanted
I know what it feels like to be cut off because I used to be the toxic one
I know the reasons people stop fucking with you.
Just like I know the reasons people don't like an evolving,
YOU.
Changing choices and hearing voices.
No, it's not mental
It's called universal.
Been working on my forgiveness and not forgetting
Letting things come and go with ease and flow as I come to my senses
Realization of thoughts and patterns that waivered in forever.
Changing your mindset is the hardest thing to do when mostly negativity has always been a part of or surrounded by you.
I haven't heard a
"hey how are you holding up since the passing of your mother"
Y'all wanna know some shady shit I wasn't even told and the fact I heard by word of mouth from another source instead of directly
This shit is sticky icky and I ain't one to usually get caught
But this is something you can't come back or walk back on
So, yea I was caught off guard

I haven't heard just a

"Hey, I'm just checking in on you?"
I'm in places Where no one can hold a space.
Now, nah
this ain't to everyone
So I say bye to negativity, block, erase, and delete anything or anyone that disrupts my peace
I'm familiar that people do change
But if the patterns always reflect the same
then there has been no Change.
That's a currency I'm not willing to exchange
So Ima let go and getting into myself
Giving to everyone else has been my biggest attribute
So I am being selfish so that I, me, we, and by we I mean the inner me can get truly acquainted.
Yet again
Take it however you desire but it's with pure intentions to pour into me and not into another source
that's my new choice

I gave so much of myself and I have nothing left for me
Can't recall a time I was ever truly happy
Fuck what you see on social media
Only a few know the truth
But I'm still authentic
Looking for nourishment
Like to the sky for the north star like my ancestors did
Believing faithfully they too are gonna be freed
Now who I gave to isn't here or around
I'm either a fool or a clown or got good at the process of eliminating
It's the latter for me
I have no words
I won't speak or match energies
I'm still Seeing my beauty
Embraced the struggles that were testimonies
If I had to burn Babylon down
I'd do it again
Ain't nothing there but ashes and everything dead
Ain't no one tells me that forgiving is never ending and the tears will flow but as time goes
They water the garden I had forgotten
So It's Time to eat
It's harvest
I'm good eating alone

I have been doing it this long
like go get dressed for a fine date, wine,
maybe a movie with pop buttery popcorn,
cozy with a blanket,
vibing and having a good time by myself
Or in nature with a good book and Ra the sun
All praises to the most high
It's the real ME season again
Nothing personal if you don't hear from me
it's just we've outgrown and the way I look and think
I love elevation
So if your elevator ain't going up
Or looking beyond our circumstances
Giving back, wanting to be of service and not be serviced
It's the patterns I see
and I stopped settling for crumbs
I deserve a platter
So Ima eat all this
plant-based nourishment

So if it offends you or makes you feel some type of way
I ain't bothered by the noise
It just reaffirms my re-evaluation and composition
I choose right by doing what brings me joy

Dating

I do not respond to baby, boo, or Bae on the first day unless after a while I'm yo lady
If you wanna get to know me how about coming up with a form of conversation
Be Sheldon or Steve Urkel. You can even be the Black Panther and I be the cat woman
This kitty will make you purr
Like Eartha Kitt
O wait that's me
I perfected that shit over the years because damn what black woman on TV you see that was the object of everyone who set their eyes on her desire
Kitt maybe my nickname but you'll never know that because you ain't talking
You bring loudness, disrespect, and multiplier convos with others while you are on the phone with ME
I will hang up on you in a heartbeat
I ain't about to sit in silence listen to your breathing while you listening to music but you supposed to be talking to me
My vernacular won't allow me to lower my bar
They said it's cold, heartless, and rude but wtf do you call all that you doing, talking to everyone every so often
I know I'm beautiful so gimme a beautiful conversation
Ppl these days
Play way too many games
Like online dating
Ur profile says you wanna chat but you really wanna duck
Your bio says casual dating but you looking for your forever
Ur bio says into all this eclectic shit that's dope but u do none of it
Wtf
Make it make sense
Make it make sense
It doesn't
It won't
U can't
My mouth can be foul but my truth is what ima give you
Take it or leave it
But I'm not no side piece I am the entire full course
I am the average female who will sit in silence with you not talking
I stopped doing that in 6th grade
I am not your previous exe so you compare me to them or think subconsciously I'm
like her when in reality you need a self-check on yourself

I'm not the one
I will read you just like it's day one and tell you everything about yourself
I am her that one
The one that's going make you aware that of what I want is this then you don't approach it like that
Facts
By the time I explain the things to you
Trust I already tapped out verbally a mentally
It's just you don't do it for me
You not boring
We all got stories but I ain't gonna sit in yours when I have to rescue me
Babygirl see you rubbed off
Bc that ain't me
U so you not getting a pet name only the name that is on your birth certificate
Unless you identify as he/she/they/them and then some
Then I will call as such but if you tell me your name is Zaddy your dismissed
Sadly but not really I'm still single
I have patience just not for bullshit

Real Shit

It's the pain that reflected my purpose

I stopped giving unnecessary lip service

Legitimacy ain't a means to intimacy

While lying in sheets that DON'T match up

Match me

100 percent

Be real enough to be your real self when you are with me

If not then expect me to leave

Dancing With the Moon

She gave her all to everyone.
Except to herself
Drawing and waiting
Wondering if the words spoken via a whisper internally to her were a gift or a curse
Written them down and the inspirations speaking yet rejecting her known philosophies
Thinking while contemplating
Awaiting for a better place within the sky where all her dreams were placed, laid, and ultimately died
She stayed when she wanted to leave but her heart didn't allow her to be
Separate from the truth she stayed while again wanting to go
She lay in a place with no one to lean on
Her final wish.... I do not know
I know she was ready to go
Grief from unhealed trauma and family drama
Secrets she took to her grave and would never tell
Giving and receiving but not receiving and accepting the love she always knew she deserved
Feeling every blow to the face while in the womb, every cry and kick
She tried to move on but love and her mixed emotions had her staying believing it was the price she had to pay
She kept it with her and she decided to change zip codes internally
As she lay on the bed with her thoughts and life being lived without her
she lost the very person she had the best connection with; herself
Denying that she was safe and yet feeling unprotected and lonely she began to fantasize about death and allow it to romanticize her thoughts
She forgot that " I forgive you" is all she needed to begin a new so she could then begin to understand her reaction to the sacrifices to herself
She delighted in her demise and no longer fought as she felt alone and no one came to visit at the bedside
She laid and life continued to pass her by and she began to wonder What will be her own life and her demise

Unable to break through the thoughts of her own life
The unhealed and masked portions that she tried to hide and run from but the more she lay the more the visions played
So the only acceptable thing she could do would be to think about her own life and that her own life as a sacrifice or was it
She laid and waited
Asked for help and no one came as life was living others and she felt especially deserted in a dire time of need
The five children she birthed seemed to be too busy to love her
However, she could not think clearly that her cries came a little too late not that they couldn't
Some just wouldn't
Others were too ill to tell her their mess to not mess with her ailing heart and mind
and so she eventually departed
Thinking of the places and people that made her feel safe.
She won her force of battle and left the fight only to leave behind a trail of tears
Laying in hospice and taking her last breathe alone
Where were her children and grandchildren?
Where were the ones she loved so much that she kept her health came last while putting them first?
Then with a light and tunnel in front of her, she lessened her grip and grasped the unknown alone
The feeling she never liked but this feeling was so real that she had no other means than to accept
So as her spirit lifted she breathed out her last breath
Although physically alone she was surrounded and waited on by all those that always believed in her and those that made her feel safe.
Her ancestors, people she called family
Lifted into the view of what she often fantasized about and ready to let go
Never telling her own story or the truths she wanted to tell
Lifted up and without looking back she walked forward with ease
Letting her own body the vessel be released
No looking back and she was carried into the light that she wanted to be in
Her final wish was to have all her kids next to her and only two know the truth but the bullet you shoot and aim at one
Be ready because there is also one for you

So lies were told and everyone left out intentionally
She said that her life would be memorialized eventually
The corpse is left to the elements and that's where the story begins to unfold and the lies told are revealed
She was intentionally left and forgotten as she was unforgiven by the ones she saw as her help except the help was disguised and was her demise and she knew it so she had to leave
Thinking about her life and all the things leaving behind realizing that again she will be memorialized with time
She said finally "I get to rest" and dance like I used to do
So she danced right into the light forever as a star in her own right
Masterminded and manipulated no one to control the narrative
Fear set in until the view of all those on the other side made her smile and feel safe again
Mom, you will forever be revered as a strong woman with many unknown weights, secrets, pain and trauma you hid
Your wishes were granted as you wrapped your mind around
TIME
Let this be known that although secrets and truths untold were left behind
Your true character and ability to uplift others even in your own time will forever be the truth
I love you
Your favorite place in nature
So yea; I love dancing with you barefoot under the moon
Mom

Grief

Cries and unanswered questions
Truths that one may know however unable to get the real story told

Wishing that things were different and had been mended before the transition
Some things are in the blood, lineage, and composition
Things that are not under one's control and aren't meant to be known
The anger will eat at you like a hungry lion
Knowing that;
This ain't it and you want a break
So you immortalize death to be with those who departed
Aware that you will then leave another without you
So to clear the truth you begin to assess who is displaying the
most
Whose at peace and who not
Lift ain't meant to be lived in regret, fear, or the departed
Celebrate their accomplishments and achievements
Knowing you did all you could do
Let the rest handle itself and heal the heart of your own
A void of a space that could never be filled
The power of forgiveness
Love transmuted to light
Anger turned into power and accomplishments and then you see
that even in death with grief
Things get better eventually
You dare to let go of what no longer belongs to you
Live on and in your truth fully aware of those watching you
In honor of the new change is mystery
So to master the mastery of embracing change
One doesn't seek revenge
Grief is cries, what ifs, but I, maybe I could have; etc
Fussing and blaming oneself is detrimental to your mental health so I advise that
you place it on paper to have it legitimatized
As with all time the pain and coping habits could diminish and as you come
up for air
Understanding that life is never your burden to bare or the choices of others
Move onward and deal with your own mental and allow it to encourage you
If you choose to
Let the burden be what it is and what it ain't
Remember that every saint was a sinner and every sinner once was a saint

Not to quote the Bible yo
I feel like we've all done shit no matter your faith background
It's just how my mind thinks and in that, I can stand
The departed are saints in their own right

Ase

Surrender

Familiar settings but a different city
Familiar people but different people
I was making progress, but it looked like regression
Nope I reply, remove it from on the side; depression
One day I was unbothered.
And I realized that my surroundings no longer moved me
Life is worth living.
I saw stagnation and honey I am meant to stand out.
I knew something was different when I cut my hair.
Started wearing lipstick.
So, I apply it, speak it, breathe it, sing it, see it.
I knew I was ready to let go.
I stopped fighting and resisting.
I kneeled and I placed my hands up to surrender.
I let go fully.
I kept my eyes, and sight looking forward.
No matter what was happening around me
That's when everything came.
Manifestations and unforeseen blessings

You can Call Her Triumphant to Surrender

No matter what you have been through or going through
You can contribute
To the life you want to have
I didn't know that until it tried to have me.
Do not allow that to be you!

The best gift you can give is the one you owe to yourself.

BE TRIUMPHNANT.

I speak because my story does not belong hidden. After all, it can also belong to another person. Maybe they needed what I wrote. I did which is why I wrote it thank you for reading it.
I hope it also helps you!

Thank you!

Oyemi

Formerly known as

Qui Michelle

www.ingramcontent.com/pod-product-compliance
Lightning Source LLC
LaVergne TN
LVHW010622100826
845148LV00014B/3075
* 9 7 8 0 5 7 8 8 9 3 9 1 4 *